THE COUNTRY DIARY
HERBAL

Hawthorn blossom

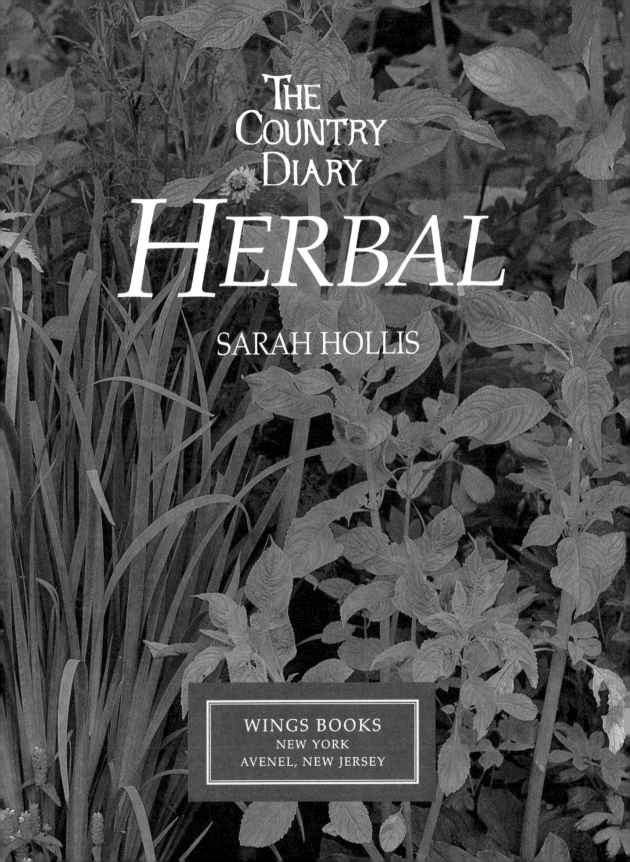

THE COUNTRY DIARY
HERBAL

SARAH HOLLIS

WINGS BOOKS
NEW YORK
AVENEL, NEW JERSEY

Title page: Golden elder in the ornamental garden.

Text copyright © 1990 by Sarah Hollis
Country Diary illustrations copyright ©1977 by Richard Webb Ltd
Country Diary copyright © 1977 by Richard Webb Ltd
Nature Notes illustrations © 1989 by Rowena Stott
Nature Notes copyright © 1989 by Rowena Stott

First published in the United States by Henry Holt and Company, Inc.,
115 West 18th Street, New York, New York 10011.
First published in Great Britain in 1990 by
Webb & Bower (Publishers) Limited.

Designed by Ron Pickless
Picture research by Anne-Marie Ehrlich

The publishers would like to thank Rowena Stott, Edith Holden's great-niece
and the owner of the original works, who has made the publication of this book possible.

This 1995 edition is published by Wings Books,
distributed by Random House Value Publishing, Inc.,
40 Engelhard Avenue, Avenel, New Jersey 07001,
by arrangement with Henry Holt and Company, Inc.

Random House
New York • Toronto • London • Sydney • Auckland

Printed and bound in China

Library of Congress Cataloging-in-Publication Data
Hollis, Sarah.
The country diary herbal / Sarah Hollis. – 1st American ed.
p. cm.
Originally published: Exeter, Devon : Webb & Bower, 1990.
Includes biographical references (p. 143).
ISBN 0-517-12292-8
1. Herbs. 2. Herb Gardening. 3. Herbs – Utilization.   I. Title.
[SB351.H5H63 1995]
635' .7–dc20   94-42942
CIP

8 7 6 5 4 3 2 1

CONTENTS

INTRODUCTION

The discovery and publication of Edith Holden's *The Country Diary of an Edwardian Lady* was one of those· happy coincidences. Her unpretentious and sensitive appreciation of the natural life all around her, perfectly complemented the recent reawakening of our interest in the tenuous balance of nature and fears for its safety. An unprecedented international success, *The Country Diary of an Edwardian Lady* and the *The Nature Notes of an Edwardian Lady* might even be said to have helped generate this new awareness of the fragility of our planet. After all, the gentle touch is frequently a more potent agent for reform than a sledgehammer.

Since *The Country Diary of an Edwardian Lady* was first published in 1977 few areas of our life have been left unaffected by an increasingly 'green' attitude to life. Those that are able to do so now fill their cars with unleaded petrol and contribute to organizations whose aim is to protect our environment or areas of great natural beauty. We are more discriminating in what we eat and drink, avoiding synthetic products or those that have been treated with chemicals. Even the large supermarket chains now offer organically grown vegetables. Attitudes to preserving good health are better informed and less cavalier; alternative medicine and natural remedies are now commonly used in preference to or in conjunction with conventional medical care.

Ivy

Sweet violet

An extraordinary change in lifestyle and attitude has taken place in the last decade. What would have been considered the wild alarmist warnings of environmentalists, crazy theories or the misguided perpetration of old wives' tales a short while ago, is now being scientifically proved correct and generally accepted. Perhaps one of the most interesting aspects is the realization that each one of us in some small way can help slow up, if not halt, our own self-destruction. Gradually, the indiscriminate worship of the great god Progress is now being overtaken by similar reverential respect for Conservation and Preservation.

One of the great charms of Edith Holden's diaries is the wonderful feeling of permanence they generate. She could wander the lanes, fields and meadows around her home, explore the moorlands of Devon and Scotland and be sure of visiting a favourite wood and finding, yet again, that violets come into flower, or admire the frothy heads of meadowsweet decorating a damp ditch. Little did she imagine the changes to come and how the flora and fauna she loved would disappear. This was engineered by what at first seemed miracles of science: the agricultural chemical warfare against disease and pests and the dubious advances in the speed of travel which, among other things, rules out the peaceful and minute observation of our surroundings. The long-term physical and emotional effects of such changes are only now revealing themselves and it is not difficult to imagine that Edith Holden would have supported any effort to return to a less polluted and natural way of life.

Yellow heartsease and common bugle

She was keenly aware of the essential role played by wild plants, as well as appreciating their beauty, and was familiar with their links with ancient customs and the past. She would use the old country names that, in the case of many herbs, describes their characteristics, or gives a clue as to how they were used. Their Latin names would often indicate their connections with ancient lore and legend. A vast number of wild plants that we now consider to be weeds, the dandelion is an example, are herbs – plants that have a medicinal or culinary use. In fact all useful plants can be defined as herbs, embracing not only those that heal and flavour, but those that nourish, dye, scent, cleanse, repel or revive.

Scientific research, though it has only just begun to scrape the suface of how and why plants can heal, is gradually proving that there is a certain amount of truth in many old wives' tales. Plants have always been used in conventional medicine but increasingly the wisdom of using the whole natural plant as opposed to a scientifically extracted part of it, is now being recognized. One of the major advantages of taking a herbal remedy rather than a pharmaceutical medicine, is that possible side-effects, often as uncomfortable as the illness itself, are avoided.

In China herbal remedies form the basis of treatment and have been prescribed with success for centuries on a large scale. This is partly due to the enormous, largely scattered peasant community and pedestrian economy. In the Western world so much of what we now consider valuable plant knowledge, and well-founded respect for their use, was confined to the scrap heap in the name of progress triggered by prosperity. Fortunately, even though recipes for cures are no longer handed down from one generation to another, the centuries-old herbals have survived intact. They still have much to offer but should be read by the layman for interest and entertainment rather than reference. Certain remedies recommended are based more on superstition, old pagan and religious festivals and beliefs than strong medical evidence.

Edith Holden herself noted and illustrated many of the medicinal, culinary and cosmetic herbs described in this herbal. It embraces not only portraits of their historic and contemporary uses but information on how they can be grown to provide a decorative and practical addition to the garden and, in their dried form, the home. It was always the most unassuming, wild, rather than exotic plants that caught her eye and her delightful paintings of these led us to appreciate their simple beauty afresh. In an age when we are seeking to resurrect and strengthen our ties with the natural world and acknowledge the vital importance of our interrelation with all its parts, it is entirely appropriate to take an equally fresh look at herbs.

May or hawthorn

The Publishers accept no responsibility for any illness arising from the misuse of these plants.

HISTORICAL BACKGROUND

How fascinating it would be know how man first experimented with plants and to hear of the origination of certain herbs being used as medicines, perfumes and cosmetics, as well as preservatives, aids to digestion and sources of food and flavouring. Ancient herbals tell us a certain amount and reveal how inextricably entangled superstition, religion, art and medicine were, but there is little information available as to how herbs became the fabric of the every-day life of early man. The animal kingdom instinctively knows what might poison or heal, but man has had to act as his own guinea pig.

We know that herbalism was practised in ancient Egypt, the herbalists relying as much on the efficacy of the contents of their medicine boxes as on the 'magical' powers of the wand or rod. Certainly, up until four hundred years before Christ was born when the Greek physician Hippocrates rejected the belief that illness was caused by supernatural powers entering the body, superstition and medicine walked hand in hand. Even when a more scientific approach was introduced to medical practice extraordinary superstitions continued to be respected. Gerard,

Daisy

in his sixteenth-century herbal, gives credence to a widely held belief by stating that he actually saw the barnacle tree on which barnacle geese were believed to grow. It may have been wishful thinking or necessity that prompted the birth of this myth, for these geese could accommodatingly be eaten on fast days, their origination being vegetable rather than animal.

Perhaps it is not so strange, for even today we believe the discovery of a four-leaf clover will bring us luck and that flowering May brought into the house bodes ill for all the inhabitants. In the seventeenth century the Doctrine of Signatures was still acknowledged by herbalists such as William Coles (1626-1662). It perpetuated the belief that every plant, by its shape, colour or individual characteristics, directed either on which part of the body it could most effectively be used or denoted the nature of the illness. *Pulmonaria officinalis* or lungwort (wort being the medieval name for herb) is an example, for the white spots on its foliage were believed to represent its usefulness in relation to diseases of the lung. Obviously many assumptions about the properties of certain plants were incorrect, but some, quite by chance, were right.

Herbs were an indispensable ingredient of early gardens. They added fragrance to the paradise gardens of Persia, perfumes being particularly highly valued in the east, and scented the formal plots made by the Romans both at home and abroad. In the first century AD a Greek physician to the Roman army, Dioscorides, wrote *De Materia Medica*, a forerunner of the herbal that was to be a respected source of plant knowledge for hundreds of years. The Roman's chief export was their sophisticated way of life and wherever they conquered they built villas and laid out formal gardens with beds edged with box or rosemary in which herbs were grown for culinary

The Monk in The Priory Garden, Lavenham.

and medicinal purposes. They introduced to Britain borage, chives, coriander, fennel, mustard, rosemary and chervil as well as vegetables such as leeks, onions, cucumbers and asparagus. At a time when the Celtic Druid priest was overseeing human sacrifice and valuing above all other plants, mistletoe and the oak (the first symbolized purification and the second was deemed to have magical powers) the Roman was treating the ill-effects of his over indulgence with infusions of herbs: ground elder for gout and fennel for indigestion. Many of the plants introduced by the Romans could only survive the climate of ancient Britain by being tended with great care. Once the Romans left, these delicate specimens were neglected and consequently lost. The Dark Ages descended and knowledge

pertaining to the use and care of plants had to seek sanctuary in the safe confines of the monasteries.

As monks travelled from one monastery to another, valuable information was exchanged, passed on by word of mouth and recorded in manuscripts that were copied – various details inevitably became distorted or embroidered. Impressively well organized and self-supporting, the monasteries were large communities, often supporting five hundred or more inhabitants. Caring for the sick was an important Christian duty and consequently the infirmary was a vital part of the whole. Though a crude form of medicine was being practised by what was known as travelling 'bone setters', it was the monk that became the first general physician.

Herbs were gathered from the wild as well as grown in small enclosed gardens, and strict rules were laid down as to when these should be harvested. Many plants have the name St John's

Herb Robert

sacristan's garden in which flowers for the church and special festivals were grown.

In the ninth century the emperor Charlemagne in his *Capitulare de Villis et Curtis*, listed over eighty plants that should be grown in a garden and the monk Walafred Strabo described in his poem *The Little Garden*, the garden of the monastery of St Gall. It was similar to a Roman garden in that it had pools and fountains and rectangular beds of herbs divided by straight paths. Strabo urges the gardener not to be lazy 'but full of zeal continuously, nor must he despise hardening his hands with toil'. He writes of plants and their uses and describes horehound as being 'bitter to the palate yet its scent is sweet. Drink horehound hot from the fire if you are poisoned by your stepmother', and recommends taking wormwood for fever and gout.

For many centuries the monastery acted as the prime source of plants and plant knowledge. Travelling monks and hospitaller orders such as the Knights Templar and Knights of St John would return from the east with new plants and remedies. Gradually, as every-day life became less hazardous and threatened by invaders, the medieval pleasure garden made its appearance.

We know considerably more about the development of the pleasure garden than earlier gardens due to the survival of illuminated manuscripts, herbals and tapestries that depict their design and describe plants grown. A small enclosed garden would stand within the castle walls, a peaceful outdoor room that was a refuge from the hurly-burly of castle life. Raised beds surrounded a small lawn dotted with flowers, (many of which we would now consider weeds) or a central fountain, water being a popular feature of these retreats. Arbours, herb alleys and turf seats were fragrant with roses, honeysuckle, camomile, pennyroyal and violets, and the beds would be planted with gilliflowers or pinks, columbines, lilies, irises and lavender. Beyond the castle walls there would be a kitchen garden, 'flowery mead', orchard and even a vineyard.

wort to this day, because they could only be gathered on that particular saint's day. There were strict rules governing the exact type of cutting tools to be used, also the time of year, day or night for harvesting and which prayer should be intoned while gathering the 'crop'. Herbs were put to many uses within the strict confines of monastery life: the cellarer needed bitter herbs such as mugwort, elder, dandelion and ground ivy to flavour the ale; the scholar monk required dye plants to colour the inks used in illuminating manuscripts; the fraterer and guest-house master needed strewing herbs to sweeten the atmosphere, for fires and to soften the tread of many feet. They were needed in the refectory, pot herbs being used to disinfect (certain herbs had minor antiseptic qualities) and flavour the often rancid meat. They added zest to a bland and limited diet and relieved its often leaden effect on the digestion. Aromatic and medicinal herbs were used by the almoner who tended the sick and dying, and the monastery chamberlain greatly valued their insect-repellent qualities. Apart from the herb garden, the monastery would have an orchard, more often than not incorporated with the cemetery and, most important, a

Religious symbolism played an important part in garden-making – flowers were considered the essence of holiness. Medieval illustrations of the Virgin frequently depict her in a garden embroidered with flowers, lilies signifying purity, roses and carnations divine love, violets humility, daisies innocence, irises royalty and apples the sorrows of this earth. Herbs and flowers were intermingled, the former now a common and necessary part of every-day life. Strewn on the floors of a dwelling, they sweetened the otherwise fetid air, were indispensable in the kitchen (the choice of vegetables being extremely limited) and were also the raw material of many home-made remedies.

By the fifteenth century there were works describing the cultivation and use of plants. These were not as before, simply copied or translated from others, but written from the author's own experience in growing and using herbs. The following are a few of the plants listed in *The Feate of Gardening* by Mayster John Gardener that was published in 1440: hyssop, woodruff, betony, borage, henbane, lavender, southernwood, tansy, thyme, violets, yarrow, mint, rue, saffron, camomile, foxgloves, centuary, agrimony, herb robert, wormwood, sage, horehound, grounsel, clary comfrey, valerian and cowslips. Like many of the books that were to follow, it was a practical treatise despite the fact that certain myths were still perpetuated.

Honeysuckle

Dr William Turner, the Dean of Wells who is known as the Father of English Botany, wrote *A New Herball* in 1551, later published in 1562 and 1568. Written in the vernacular, it was the first book to describe many English native plants. In

Rose-bay willow herb

1597 John Gerard, gardener to Queen Elizabeth I's Lord High Treasurer Lord Burghley, wrote what has become one of the best known of all herbals. The foundation for Gerard's book was a manuscript by a Flemish botanist, Rembert Dodeons. Gerard plagiarized this manuscript along with a number of other foreign herbals. But he also wrote extensively about the several hundred plants he grew in his own nursery at Holborn and from knowledge gleaned on his travels abroad. Its revision and updating by Thomas Johnson in 1633 further increased its popularity.

In 1629 John Parkinson, apothecary to James I, wrote his *Paradisi in Sole Paradisus Terrestris* which described plants then in cultivation. His *Theatrum Botanicum: the Theatre of Plants: or an Universal and Complete Herbal,* published in 1640, was directed specifically at the herbalist. The famous herbalist, Nicholas Culpeper, published his 'The English Physician' in 1652 and this broke new ground for it was written as much for the people as the specialist, which far from pleased the College of Physicians. Though Culpeper subscribed to astrological beliefs and old-fashioned superstitions, he was not above inveighing against Gerard and Parkinson. In the introduction to the book, he complains that they never 'gave one wise reason for what they wrote and so did nothing else but train up young novices in Physic in the School of tradition, and teach them just as a parrot is taught to speak'. Botany and medicine were breaking new ground and beginning to be treated as separate sciences. Consequently eagles' feathers thrust into the ground could no longer be relied upon to ward off frost, nor could the watering-in of seeds with wine necessarily add to a plant's strength.

The relative security of the Tudor period saw the garden grow in size and ornamentation. Its layout frequently became as much the concern of the architect as the house, and it quietly evolved into a vehicle by which an owner's good taste and standing in society could be assessed. Knot

Creeping loose-strife

In Tudor England herbs were still an important ingredient of every-day life and no garden would have been complete without them. The atmosphere of a dwelling still needed sweetening with strewing herbs, nosegays or 'tussie mussies', and they were indispensable in the kitchen and still room. They added zest to home-made wines and vinegars, flavoured puddings, pottages and 'sallets'. Herbs were the forerunner of the salad and being made of ten or twenty ingredients rather than a paltry two or three were infinitely more imaginative than their modern equivalent.

The seventeenth-century diarist John Evelyn believed that the making of a 'sallet' was an art, that it must be finely tuned to the mood and character of those who were to consume it. They were made of roots, often cut into fanciful shapes, stalks, buds, leaves and the flowers of plants. He wrote: 'In the Composure of a Salid, every plant came in to bear its part, without being over-power'd by some Herb of a stronger taste, so as to endanger the native Sapor and Vertue of the vert; but fall into their places, like the Notes of Music in which there shall be nothing harsh or grating'. Sage, elder flowers, nasturtiums, violets and gilliflowers were all used, the dressing being made, as today, from a combination of sugar, pepper, salt, mustard, vinegar and oil and the yolk of an egg. In the still room perfumed washing balls, pomanders, vinegars, syrups and conserves were made. Rose, balm, rosemary and lavender waters were produced and whole flowers or delicate petals were candied.

gardens, a pattern of low, often evergreen hedges, were popular features of the period, their design frequently displaying the family emblem, or echoing the intricate plaster work of a ceiling in the house. Usually placed where they could be admired with ease from an upstairs window, knot gardens were composed of low hedges of germander, hyssop, savory, thrift and santolina or cotton lavender.

As more and more elaborate features such as topiary, raised walks, mounts, summer and banqueting houses, painted and carved wooden trellis work, rails and heraldic beasts crept into the garden, the vegetables were relegated to a separate garden to make room for the exciting new plants introduced from abroad. The New World yielded plants such as the evening primrose and a herb that the American Indians called *picelt*: thought to have great healing properties, it came to be known as tobacco.

The design of the garden became increasingly intricate up until the mid-eighteenth century. The formal walled and sectioned gardens of the Stuarts were, on Charles II's return from exile, altered to resemble the autocratic and symmetrical gardens of the French gardener designer, le Nôtre. Sophisticated parterres, paths, fountains and elegant architectural features banished the humble pot and medicinal herb to the kitchen, or to one of the newly founded physic gardens. It

Seed vessels of rose-bay willow herb

Opposite
The arbour seat in the Tudor Garden, Southampton.

was in such gardens, first seen in Oxford in 1621 and in Chelsea in 1673, that the healing properties of herbs were researched – the divisions between art, botany, medicine and science becoming ever more clearly defined. This increasing isolation from the mainstream of medical thinking plus the increasing quantity of exotic herbs and spices being imported into the country and the use of leeches rather than a herbal infusion or poultice, gradually eroded the humble herb's position in life.

In 1737, the Swede Carolus Linnaeus laid down a new classification of plants in his *Genera Plantarum*, a great advance that was to put to an end the practise of calling a single plant by several different names. This important milestone in the history of botany came about, ironically, just as 'Capability' Brown was to embark on his uniquely successful career as a landscape gardener. He somehow persuaded hundreds of clients to do away with their formal gardens and replace them with deceptively 'natural', flowerless landscapes. Away went the Dutch influenced William and Mary gardens spotted with fantastical topiary, and the intricate, work-intensive gardens laid out during Queen Anne's reign by London and Wise, who were the fashionable garden-makers and the nurserymen of the day. Highly cultivated, even ostentatious gardens were to reappear during the Victorian era, but it was the exotic, tender and half-hardy cultivated plants that held sway and not the unsophisticated native beauties. It took the eccentric William Robinson and his energetic advocacy of wild flowers and gardening, and the intensely practical, but also artistic, Gertrude Jekyll to reawaken an interest in herb gardening.

Robinson in his book *The English Flower Garden*, published in 1883, poured scorn on what he called the 'pastry cook' garden-making style of the Victorians. While Miss Jekyll's books inspired a new appreciation of the simple cottage garden and the herbs, wild hedgerow and woodland plants that had been neglected for far too long. The cottage gardens painted by Helen Allingham during this period, in which hollyhocks jostled with columbines, cornflowers and cabbages, represented a delightful idyll that has remained popular to this day.

The fads and fashions of the times, many inspired by the Arts and Crafts Movement, were not dissimilar to those of today. Hand-made rather than manufactured goods were welcomed and the natural or traditional well-crafted look was much in vogue. Herbs were once again reinstated in the garden, both as ornamental and practical plants, and there was renewed interest in their various uses. Herbal remedies were enjoying a revival, especially in America where the self-sufficient Shakers sect produced and sold medicinal and culinary herbs in vast quantities. They were no longer considered an ineffective mix of magic and ancient lore and the plants themselves ceased being considered purely 'weed-like' and were used to make decorative herb gardens.

Eleanour Sinclair Rohde (1880–1950), who grew and wrote extensively about old-fashioned herbs, herbals and garden history, did much in Britain to promote an interest as did Mrs Grieve who wrote the impressively comprehensive *A Modern Herbal* in 1931. The book was edited by Mrs Leyel. It was Mrs Leyel who went on to open the first of what was to become a chain of Culpeper shops which sold herbal remedies, cosmetics and other herbal products, as well as offer consultations. Eleanour Sinclair Rohde was a member of the advisory committee. The energy and interest of these three women ensured that valuable historic information would not become extinct. The unavailability of many chemical medicines during the First and Second World War, and cessation of imports of herbs and spices from abroad, boosted interest further. A good number of herb nurseries, such as the one started by Dorothy Hewer in Kent in 1926, began to grow herbs on a commercial basis. The English climate was conducive to producing herbs whose flavour and essential oil were of an extremely high quality.

The use of herbs on the Continent, especially by the peasant community, had never really died out – contrary to the situation in Britain. They were an essential ingredient of many local and national dishes, a cheap source of medicinal remedies and disinfectant and a preservative of food in generally more extreme temperatures. As foreign travel became easier and cheaper, so did culinary knowledge and tastes change – brown windsor soup, liver and bacon and rice pudding, soon being usurped by more exciting fare.

Today herbs play as important a role as they did in their medieval heyday, though it is scientific proof and personal taste, rather than myths and legends, that now guide our preferences. They have crept into every room of the house in some guise, a large proportion of commercial household products, from shampoos to floor polish, being scented by or containing an extract from some herb or other. The new 'green' outlook on life demands that many consumer products should be, or at least appear to be, 'natural', the name of a herb or the words 'home', 'farmhouse', or 'country' featuring widely. Fresh, home-grown, or dried herbs are a common ingredient of the contemporary kitchen and infusions or 'tisanes' are fast becoming a popular, tannin- and caffeine-free, alternative to tea and coffee. As Culpeper himself said 'A good cook is half a physician'. Modern chemical drugs are now regarded with greater caution, their side-effects often causing an unwelcome chain of reactions and lowering of resistance. Organically grown foodstuffs and alternative medicine which embraces herbalism is no longer considered an eccentric last resort, the desire to live a natural, healthy and stress-free life having brought our story full circle.

Juniper berries

GROWING HERBS

Growing instructions for individual herbs can be found in the A–Z Herbal section

Herbs are generally the most accommodating of plants to grow, a great number will flourish on poor soil and are resistant to disease, their one enemy being heavy, badly drained soil. For best results in the garden plant herbs in conditions which most closely resemble their wild, uncultivated originals. Aromatic herbs such as rosemary, which originated on the dry, sun-baked terrain of the Mediterranean regions, should do well on a sunny rockery, an area of scree, or free-draining gravelly soil. Others might languish in brilliant sunshine and therefore enjoy partial or complete shade; many varieties relish moist or even marshy ground; others suit the more strict confines of a pot or positively thrive, like the houseleek, in the mean conditions offered by a crack in a wall. To achieve satisfactory results it pays to investigate the individual needs of each plant.

GENERAL RULES AND HINTS FOR GROWING HERBS

Avoid over manuring herbs, especially aromatics, as this will promote a great deal of top growth that is devoid of scent and flavour. A liquid seaweed manure is recommended and a sprinkling of hydrated lime in autumn will aid the breaking down of organic matter and so improve the quality of growth. A dose of bone meal or organic manure can be given in spring. If a shrub or perennial herb should die do not plant a replacement in the same spot as the ground will be exhausted of the necessary nutrients. Ideally, organic growing methods are recommended as they ensure that the herbs are kept chemical and pollutant free. If they are attacked by aphids use derris dust or pyrethrum powder for these are natural insecticides. When buying herbs always choose specimens with a good root system as well as top growth and tease out the roots before planting or they will become 'balled', thus preventing or stunting growth.

GROWING HERBS FROM SEED

Buy seed from one of the specialist or large commercial seed companies. Growing from seed is the most economical way to raise plants; set the seed in trays under glass or plant out directly into the ground. Resist the temptation to sow too early in spring, especially outside when the seed could be damaged by a late frost. Fresh ripe seed of perennials such as lovage, should be planted in autumn and plants whose foliage is valued, such

Foxglove

as parsley, should be sown *in situ*, as transplanting causes early flowering. When sowing inside fill pots or trays with a soil- or peat-based compost and firm down. Sow the seed thinly, cover with a fine layer of soil and water. A sheet of glass or Perspex, to retain moisture and another of newspaper, to block out the light, should then be placed over the pot or tray. Continue to check if the seeds are germinating and remove the glass and newspaper at the first signs of life. When the seedlings have produced two or three leaves, prick out or transplant into trays or small pots. Grow on until they are ready to plant outside, taking great care beforehand to ensure that the plants are well 'hardened off', ie, that they have been gradually acclimatized to the outside temperature.

When sowing outside prepare the soil by raking to a fine tilth and sprinkle seeds thinly down a drill and cover with a thin layer of soil, then water. Keep weed free and if seedlings grow too close together, thin out by removing smaller plants so that each plant will flourish.

TAKING CUTTINGS FROM STEMS AND ROOTS

Cuttings should only be taken from healthy vigorous plants, using a **sharp** knife. Soft stem cuttings are taken in spring and summer. Cut a 3–6in (7.5–15cm) stem, just below a leaf bud where the material is hardier and more resistant to rot. Strip the leaves off the lower half, dip the end into hormone rooting powder and insert around the edges of pots of well-firmed compost. Cover with a plastic bag to retain moisture and place in the shade. If given heat from below, as in a propagating unit, the cuttings will root more readily.

Heeled cuttings are side shoots from lower down the stem. The shoot is pulled off the branch taking with it a 'heel' or flick of wood from the main stem. Strip all leaves and buds from the lower half of the cutting and plant as above.

Hardwood cuttings, taken from deciduous trees and shrubs, are taken in the autumn and early spring before bud-burst. Take a shoot that is one season old and cut as near to where it joins the main branch as possible. This is the most viable part of the material. Cut straight across the bottom of the stem, the top on a slant just above a bud. Place in a deep trench lined with a thin layer of sand, only a small proportion of the cutting appearing above the soil.

Root cuttings are taken in the winter and autumn when the plant is dormant. Cut 3in (7.5cm) lengths of healthy root (identify the top by cutting straight, the bottom on a slant) and place right side up vertically (or horizontally if the plant is thin rooted) in a box of potting compost and cover thinly. Water, cover with glass and paper and place in the shade. Elecampane, comfrey, marshmallow and mulleins can be propagated in this way.

ROOT DIVISION AND LAYERING

One further method of propagating fast-growing plants that are apt to deteriorate from the centre is by root division. Dig up the whole herb and, using two forks, wrench apart. Discard the centre and plant the outer roots and keep well watered until established.

Layering is an ideal way of propagating herbs such as sage and thyme that are apt to get straggly and woody towards the centre. Peg down horizontally into the ground only allowing the healthy stems of the parent plant to grow. Do not cut free until an adequate root system has formed and shoots have been thrown up. Then sever from the parent plant and transplant to required growing position.

HARVESTING

Although there is no longer any need to intone prayers, or gather only certain herbs on a

Overleaf
Fields of fragrant lavender.

Common ivy

particular date, there are rules to be followed.

When gathering from the wild be sure that the herbs are uncontaminated by any pollutant. If on, or near, farmland they might have been sprayed with pesticide and if by the roadside they may have absorbed lead from the atmosphere. Always ask permission to gather herbs on private land and be sure that your plant identification is correct. It is relatively easy to mistake one wild plant for another, so always be on guard for some plants are deadly poisonous.

The majority of herbs can be harvested in early to late summer. They should be cut mid-morning, when the dew has dried but the sun is not yet at its hottest, great care being taken not to damage the material in any way. Seeds are gathered when they are ripe, the seed head, still on the stem, should be placed in a brown paper bag and hung upside down in a warm dry area. Rhizomes and roots are harvested in early spring or late autumn, washed, cut into pieces and then dried. If it is the foliage of a herb that is required, this is at its best just before the plant flowers. If the whole herb is to be used, gather just as the flowers are about to open. All material should be dried as quickly as possible to preserve the special properties. Most plants contain seventy per cent moisture and should weigh one eighth of their original weight when dry, and crumble easily

when handled. The ideal place in which to dry herbs is in an airing cupboard, dry outhouse or attic. They should be hung in bunches, spread on trays of netting stretched over a wooden frame or laid out on newspaper. Turning them regularly during the first few days will ensure they dry evenly. It is essential that they are shaded from sunlight, for it will sap their colour and virtues, and that dry air is allowed to circulate. A low oven, no hotter than 33C/90F and with the door left slightly open, or a microwave, can be used to dry the herbs. Experiment with a small quantity of the material first, taking note of the fact that large-foliaged herbs will take longer to dry than smaller varieties.

STORAGE

Once dried, the foliage or flowers can be carefully stripped off the stalks and then stored in airtight jars. These should be placed out of the light and labelled and dated – the dried material should not be kept for longer than a year. Do not use plastic containers as these have an adverse effect on the material. Certain herbs, especially those to be used in cooking, such as parsley, can be chopped and stored dry or in ice cubes in the freezer.

HERBAL PREPARATIONS

The following are examples of herbal prepara-tions that can be made easily at home, there are a number of others but they require sophisticated equipment and pharmaceutical expertise.

A FEW RULES

Herbal medicines are surprisingly potent and no remedy should be taken over a long period or the safe dose exceeded. If there is any doubt as to the suitability of the herbal medicine to the complaint a qualified practitioner should be consulted. This cannot be stressed strongly enough. Always use a stainless-steel knife to cut material and a stainless-steel or enamel saucepan with a well-fitting lid. Measuring jugs and spoons are useful, other essential equipment will include a funnel, pieces of muslin, a nylon sieve or coffee filter papers, a pestle and mortar and numerous labels. Glass jars and bottles will be needed for storing herbal products but avoid using metal lids on these as they can have an adverse effect on the contents. Do not keep decoctions or infusions for longer than twelve hours as they deteriorate quickly and always store herbal preparations in the fridge. Use pure water and when re-heating do so in a bain-marie or a heat-proof glass basin set over a saucepan of boiling water. Do not boil flowers. Only half the quantities stated should be used when making herbal remedies for children.

INFUSION

This process can be compared to making tea, as boiling water is poured on to the finely chopped herb and left to infuse for up to fifteen minutes. Ensure that any vessel used has a lid to prevent evaporation of the valuable properties. Strain through fine muslin, coffee filter paper or a nylon sieve before drinking. The percentage of herb to water is usually 1oz (28g) of fresh herb or ½oz (14g) dried (1oz (28g) of dried herb being twice as strong as that of fresh) to 1pt (600ml/2½ cups) water. The infusion can be taken lukewarm or cold. The recommended dosage is 3tbs (45ml/¼ cup) taken three times a day before meals.

DECOCTION

This method is used to extract the beneficial substances from dried chopped roots, rhizomes, crushed seeds and bark. These are placed in a saucepan of cold water, soaked for a short period and then slowly brought to the boil and simmered for about ten to fifteen minutes – always ensure there is a lid on the saucepan. Leave the herb to steep until the water goes cold and then strain. Proportions of the herb to the water are usually 1oz (28g) of the herb to 1pt (600ml/2½cups) of water and the recommended dosage is 3tbs (45ml/¼ cup) before meals, three times a day.

POULTICE AND COMPRESS

These can be made with fresh or dried herbs that have been made into a paste with a small quantity of hot water or, in the case of dried herbs, with cider vinegar. The paste is wrapped in muslin or gauze and applied to the skin. The poultice, like the compress, should be kept warm. The latter is simply a piece of material soaked in a warm infusion or decoction and applied to the relevant area of the body.

COSMETIC PREPARATIONS

Various herbs can be used for cosmetic prepara-tions but it is essential to match the herb to the skin type and test, on a small area of skin, for any allergic reaction before use. Certain herbs such as marigold, yarrow or lady's mantle have astringent properties and are therefore ideal for oily skins; sweet violet, marshmallow and elder flower are emollients and therefore kind to a dry skin. Others such as nettles, rosemary and chamomile make good hair conditioners and rinses, or in the case of soapwort, a chemical-free shampoo. A wide range of herbal extracts added to the water make a soothing or refreshing bath or, when mixed with yoghurt or oatmeal, a beneficial face-pack.

Hips of villous rose

COMPANION PLANTS

A companion plant has a beneficial effect on the health and vigour of its neighbour, and it will attract or repel insects that might either pollinate or damage plants growing nearby. Especially useful in the fruit and vegetable garden, many of these plants release from their roots, foliage or flowers, a repellent gas or aroma, while others feed or condition the soil.

Certain herbs can be used to make cheap, organic fertilizers and pesticides. Comfrey is a valuable source of potash and nitrogen and can be put to good use on the compost heap. Nettles are rich in iron and if a couple of handfuls are soaked in a bucket of rain water for a few weeks, they produce what old-fashioned gardeners would call a 'weak tea' feed that can then be watered on young plants. The foliage of garlic or onions, when used as a plant spray, will ward off disease. Elder leaves have proved particularly successful at keeping aphids at bay: soak the foliage in water as above, adding some washing-up liquid to the strained mixture to ensure that it does not simply run off the surface of the plant.

Borage planted among strawberries will increase the crop. Chamomile, the 'plant physician', when grown beside a sickly culinary plant, will stimulate growth and improve its flavour. Chives, grown at the foot of an apple tree, will prevent scab and, planted around roses, will ward off blackspot. A clove of garlic planted at the base of a rose will keep it free from greenfly.

Fragrant herbs such as sage, rosemary, thyme, marjoram, chives and hyssop will keep the vegetable garden healthy, either promoting growth or, as in the case of hyssop, by attracting the cabbage white butterfly and maintaining its attention.

Marigolds – French, African and pot – are superb at repelling insects, both above and below ground. Pot (*calendula*) and French marigolds (*Tagetes patula*) and basil planted in the greenhouse along with tomatoes, or beside other plants or rows of vegetables, will repel whitefly, flea beetles and aphids. The roots of African marigolds (*Tagetes erecta*) exude a substance that effectively combats the spread of couch grass, ground elder, ivy and horsetail.

Mint repels cabbage grubs and flies but, being a notoriously invasive plant, should be grown in pots and moved to wherever it is needed. Branches can also be picked and spread in between rows of cabbages and other brassicas. The scent of mint is disliked by mice and rats and when the leaves are rubbed on the skin it wards off mosquitoes and fleas. Bunches hung in the kitchen or a doorway will keep flies at bay. Nasturtiums protect fruit trees from aphids and keep a greenhouse free of whitefly. Parsley and garlic are said to improve the scent of roses when planted around trees or bushes.

The following herbs are good insect repellents, and bunches hung in the larder or kitchen will ward off flies: mints, rosemary, rue, southernwood, thyme, tansy and feverfew. The dried and powdered flowers of pyrethrum (feverfew has similar properties) make a strong insect repellent that can be used in the house and outdoors.

Oil of lavender, an infusion of chamomile or the leaves of elder or wormwood will protect against insect bites when rubbed on the skin.

The most frequently used moth-repellent herbs are lavender, rosemary, santolina, wormwood or southernwood (also known by the old French name *garde robe*). These can be dried and used in sachets, or branches can simply be hung or placed between protective pieces of material in drawers and cupboards.

Opposite
Country kitchen garden.

Small tortoiseshell
and stinging nettle

Rosemary wards off carrot fly, as do onions and, most conveniently, carrots in turn repel the onion fly. Being such complementary neighbours it is advisable to grow them side by side.

Rue, with its sharp, bitter, odour, repels insects most successfully. Either fresh or dried and then reduced to a powder it can be scattered around vegetables as an insect repellent. It associates well with raspberries and mint though is anathema to basil, for when not killing it off completely, it is thought to make it toxic.

Sage repels insects and generally promotes the health of neighbouring plants. Savoury, both winter and summer, is an excellent companion plant to runner and broad beans. It repels aphids but attracts bees and other pollinating insects. Rue is harmful to brassicas, and chamomile; mint, rosemary and thyme are harmful to potatoes.

Stinging nettles promote growth. They are rich in trace elements and minerals, which they return to the soil when they die down. As well as being a source of plant food they are a good natural pesticide against greenfly and blackfly and make excellent 'food' for the compost heap. If the gardener can curb his natural instinct to keep his garden weed free, he would be well advised to allow nettles to grow between the soft fruit canes and bushes as they will, like the foxglove, improve the size and flavour of the crop. Admittedly fruit picking then becomes a devilish job!

AGRIMONY

Botanical name: Agrimonia eupatoria
Alternative common name(s): Aaron's rod, church steeples, money in both pockets, cockeburr, sticklewort
Part(s) used: Leaves and flowers
Description: A lightly scented perennial, agrimony grows between 1-3ft (up to 1m) high, in ditches, along lanes, on the outskirts of woods and in meadows. It is common on the chalk and limestone uplands of Britain and is a native of Europe and Asia. Its red stems bear pinnate leaves similar to those of the strawberry, divided into three parts, with toothed edges and downy, grey undersides. The yellow flowers are borne on terminal spikes, hence the name church steeples. These tiny rose-like flowers leave behind a burr-like seed, hence the alternative name cockeburr.

The botanical Latin name *Agrimonia* comes from the Greek word *Argemone* meaning cataract; the Greeks believed that the plant had special power to heal eye complaints. The name *eupatoria* is derived from the Persian king, Mithridates Eupator of Pontus, who studied plants and their medical properties. Defeated by Pompey in 63BC he had no choice but to commit suicide and, according to legend, he swallowed poisonous plant extract. His efforts, despite his knowledge of plants were unsuccessful. Over the years he had unwittingly built up an immunity to their toxic effects and, in the end, he resorted to a more conventional contemporary form of suicide, he fell on his sword.

Included in the Anglo Saxon 'Salve' as a medicinal herb, Agrimony was thought to be effective in removing warts and treating snake bites and wounds. It was also thought to ward off the devil! It was classed as a 'simple', a herb that could be used as a remedy in its own right. Mixed with other herbs it was a well-known ingredient of a potion called 'Arquebus Water'. This was used to heal wounds inflicted by the lethal arquebus hand gun, a weapon used by the Yeoman of the Guard during the Middle Ages.

Common agrimony

Today in Germany the potion is used in a sophisticated form to treat gallstones and cirrhosis of the liver, while in China it is a treatment for excessive bleeding and in France it is a cure for bed-wetting.

An infusion of the dried flowers and leaves makes a good gargle or mouthwash, helps clear the blood, freshens the breath, soothes sore gums and, as a footbath, has proved to be a cure for athlete's foot. An infusion of the leaves alone can also be used to treat bruising. The infusion is made using either ½oz (14g) of dried herb or a handful of fresh herbs to which is added 1pt (600ml/2½cups) of boiling water. In the sixteenth century John Gerard commented in his herbal that 'A decoction of the leaves is good for them that have naughty livers'. It is certainly known to aid digestion and has a reputation as a treatment for jaundice.

Cultivation: Sow the seed in the desired flowering position or propagate by root division in the spring or autumn. It likes a well-drained sunny position but will tolerate some shade.

Harvest: The leaves for drying should be picked before the flowers have bloomed and the flowers well before the seed heads have formed. The flowers and leaves can be used fresh or dried.

ALOE Curacao/Socotrine/Cape

Botanical name(s): Aloe vera, A. perryi, A. ferox
Alternative common name(s): First-aid plant, medicine plant
Part(s) used: Bitter juice and gel from leaves
Description: A large succulent plant, aloe is a perennial that despite being a native of the tropics can be grown as a houseplant or in a greenhouse in temperate climes. A member of the lily family, it has thick, fleshy, sword-shaped leaves that have prickly margins and spikes. These surround a single stem bearing a raceme of bell-like red, yellow or orange flowers like a rosette. The flowers are similar to those of the red hot poker, *Kniphofia.* The aloe can produce flowers throughout the main part of the year.

Revered by the Muhammadans as a religious symbol, a species of aloe whose Arabic name is *saber* was traditionally planted at the foot of a grave. Translated the name means 'patience', a quality that was put to the test during the long wait between burial and resurrection. Known to have been grown on the island of Socotra and used medicinally since the fourth century BC there is mention in an Anglo-Saxon leech book of aloe being prescribed to Alfred the Great by the Patriarch of Jerusalem.

Once familiar and abhorred by many as the bitter ointment applied to the finger tips to prevent nails from being bitten, aloe is now a common ingredient of cosmetic preparations, particularly shampoos. The gel that is extracted from the succulent leaves, as opposed to the juice

which is obtained from cutting their base, is a valuable healing agent and the one in most common usage. It will improve the condition of brittle, dry hair and, used as a lotion, will rejuvenate the skin, reduce wrinkles and stimulate the circulation. The juice from the leaves can be used as a purgative but it must be mixed with other subjects to prevent it from causing sudden, intestinal pain. Only use it sparingly as it can cause haemorrhoids. Used externally, the freshly expressed gel from the leaf has remarkable regenerative powers. It will speed the healing of burns, cuts and wounds, though care must always be taken not to use the outer skin or green part of the leaf as this could cause irritation.

Cultivation: Propagate in a warm greenhouse from seed sown in sandy soil and maintain a temperature of 70F (21C). When mature keep lightly watered and stand outside during the summer months, but the plants will have to be kept inside during the winter.

Harvest: Cut the leaves to extract the gel. The juice from the base of the leaves is best extracted and administered professionally.

ANGELICA

Botanical name: Angelica archangelica
Alternative common name(s): Root of the Holy Ghost
Part(s) used: Roots, leaves and seeds
Description: Growing up to 6ft (1.8m) high, angelica has stout, hollow, stems and long fleshy roots. A biennial – and a perennial if the flower heads are cut before producing seed – it is strongly aromatic and has long triangular and dentate leaves. The attractive flowers are spherical-shaped umbels of greenish white, borne from summer to autumn.

The herb has an ancient history, was dedicated to heathen gods and featured in pagan festivals. It was considered an antidote to poisons and a remedy for infectious diseases, particularly the plague. There are several different schools of thought concerning the origin of its name: one belief is that an angel appeared to a monk and told him how it could be used to cure the plague;

Pl. 108.

Angélique archangélique.

Hoegaart del. et sculp.

Angelica

another is that it comes into flower on the old saints day of Michael the Archangel.

The seeds are used in the making of vermouth and chartreuse, and the fresh leaves of the plant, stewed with rhubarb or gooseberries, effectively soften the tart flavour of these acidic fruits. The dried leaves can be used in an infusion that has a flavour similar to that of China tea and the fresh leaves and their ribs are a tasty addition to a salad, one that is often mistaken for celery. Of course, the most familiar derivative of angelica are the candied stalks which are used to decorate cakes and puddings. The popularity of this confection, once such a familiar sight, now seems to be on the wane.

To candy angelica cut the stems in 2-3in (5-7.5cm) lengths, boil, drain and peel off the tough outer skin. Re-boil the stems which gradually turn green, then drain and dry. Make a syrup of equal quantities of water and sugar and after boiling this for eight minutes plunge in the angelica stems and simmer until they are clear. Drain and cool. The process of boiling in the syrup can be repeated several times if the stems have not absorbed sufficient sugar. The candied stems should then be stored somewhere cool in an airtight container.

An infusion of the dried roots (the strongest part of the plant), seeds or fresh or dried leaves can be taken to relieve the effects of a heavy cold, soothe a cough, relieve bronchitis and also act as an expectorant. Angelica is particularly well known for the calming effect it has on the digestion and for its ability to allay flatulence. The infusion should be taken in 1 dessert-spoon (10ml/2½tsp) doses three or four times a day and can be sweetened with honey or flavoured with the zest or a slice of lemon.

A striking, architectural plant, it is an eye-catching sight growing wild along roadside banks, though it should not be ruled out as a handsome addition to the cultivated ornamental or herb garden. The subtle colouring of its flowers can be used to highlight livelier subjects and its height will create a point of interest, but when transplanting a small young plant be sure to give it plenty of space.

Cultivation: Sow fresh seed *in situ* in the late summer or autumn, preferably in damp soil and in light shade. If it is prevented from flowering it will live for several years, if it does flower treat as a biennial and re-sow each year.

Harvest: The stems, seeds and leaves should be gathered in June or July and the root during the plant's first autumn, before it becomes damaged. The seeds, leaves and root can be dried, the latter as quickly as possible so that it does not lose its potency.

BALM

Botanical name: Melissa officinalis
Common name(s): Cure-all, lemon balm, sweet balm
Part(s) used: Herb
Description: The seventeenth-century diarist John Evelyn firmly believed that 'Balm is sovereign for the brain, strengthening the memory and power-fully chasing away melancholy' which alone should justify its cultivation. Used as a herb tea it was said to promote longevity, especially in the form of what was known as Carmelite tea. This is an infusion of balm spiced with nutmeg, angelica root and lemon peel. A doctor to Nero's army, Dioscorides, noted its healing powers when used as a dressing for wounds; it was also considered an indispensable medicinal herb in the gentlewoman's still room.

A native of central and southern Europe, North Africa and West Asia it has been grown in this country for centuries. A perennial with heart-shaped, tooth-edged, leaves and square stems, it grows to about 2ft (60cm) tall, the whole has a refreshing lemon scent when crushed, hence the common name lemon balm. The white or pale yellow flowers appear from June to October and are borne from the axils of the leaves. There is an attractive variegated variety, with golden yellow and green leaves that is well worth including in the ornamental garden, but all balms need watching as they are apt to spread fast and swamp their neighbours.

It should certainly be planted by bee hives as these industrious insects adore it. *Melissa* is Greek for bee and it is said that if the hive is rubbed down with balm, or it is planted beside the hives, it will attract new members to the colony, contain those that are restless and act as a scented beacon to those returning to the community.

Once used to treat people with hysterics and frayed nerves, balm is known for its soothing, cooling and healing powers; the volatile oil is also known to have antibacterial qualities. Aromatherapists use it to treat skin disorders such as eczema, whereas an infusion of the fresh leaves, 1oz (28g) to 1pt (600ml/2½cups) of water, is an excellent remedy for the first signs of a cold or influenza, as it promotes perspiration. The infusion will also soothe a troublesome digestion, allay flatulence, soften the skin and make a fragrant and relaxing addition to the bath.

With a zest of lemon and sweetened with honey a cold infusion can make a delicious and refreshing summer drink, and the chopped leaves add a tang to salads, stuffings or cream cheeses. They also act as a convenient soothing agent when rubbed on an insect bite.

Balm, being so easy to grow, is a must for those who make pot-pourri or herbal sleep cushions as it can make up the base of the mixture. In former times it was a favourite strewing herb and Parkinson wrote 'The Herb without all is an excellent help to comfort the heart as the very smell may induce any so to believe'.

Cultivation: Sow the seed in April or May. It is very tiny so simply press it on to the soil in trays. It can also be propagated by root division. An accommodating plant, it will tolerate most soils but its scent will be stronger if grown on moist fertile ground. A sunny position produces the best results.

Harvest: If the leaves are to be dried for future use pick before the plant has flowered, though the fresh or frozen leaves and flowers have a more powerful aroma and flavour due to the volatile oils not having been allowed to evaporate.

BASIL

Botanical name: Ocimum basilicum
Common name(s): Sweet basil, common basil, garden basil, herb royal

Part(s) used: Herb

Description: The warm pungent aroma and flavour of basil, make it one of the best loved of all culinary herbs. Growing up to 2ft (60cm) tall, it has ovate broad leaves that are grey-green beneath and smooth and shiny above. Always cool to the touch they are dotted with tiny oil cells that gives the herb its strong flavour and scent. The somewhat insignificant white to purplish flowers appear in whorls on terminal racemes from summer to autumn. These should be pinched out to promote growth and retain the warm clove flavour of the leaves. There are several different varieties such as the 6in (15cm) high dwarf bush basil *O. minimum* which though smaller is hardier; there is another variety that sports decorative purple foliage.

It is thought that its common name may well derive from the Greek word for king, *basileus*. Perhaps the herb was traditionally fed to or prescribed to royal personages, or was held in such high esteem that it was considered a herb fit for kings. Many legends and fables have attached themselves to basil over the centuries, the herb being revered in some tales but considered truly evil in others. Certain old herbals tell of its close association with scorpions, indeed it was widely believed that it could transform itself into this deadly creature. In the Middle Ages many believed that basil could only be cultivated by a beautiful woman; it was also given and received as a token of romantic love.

Most highly valued in its country of origin, India, basil or *tulasi* is sacred to the Hindu gods Krishna and Vishnu and a leaf of the herb is always placed on the breast of a dead Hindu. It is grown outside temples and a plant is kept in the house, not only because it is considered a holy plant but also because it acts as an effective disinfectant and insect repellent.

Taken as an infusion the dried or fresh leaves of basil will act as a remedy for stomach complaints such as vomiting or cramps and will soothe the digestion and prevent flatulence. Though cooling and calming as a medicinal herb it is valued more as a culinary herb, its popularity having increased greatly over the last decade. A herb traditionally used to flavour turtle soup, it is now well known as an excellent accompaniment to tomatoes and consequently many Italian dishes. There is nothing more palatable or evocative of a Mediterranean holiday than a tomato salad dressed with virgin olive oil and garnished with chopped basil leaves.

Another favourite is the Italian pesto sauce, preferably served with fresh pasta.

Pesto sauce
4oz (100g/1 cup) of fresh basil leaves (preferably from a flowering plant)
1tbs lightly roasted pine nuts
3oz (75g/1 cup) of Parmesan cheese
6tbs of olive oil
2 large cloves of garlic
Salt and pepper

Blend the basil, pine nuts and garlic to a pulp then add, alternately, a tablespoon of oil and then of cheese until all is well blended. Flavour with salt and pepper and stir into freshly cooked pasta.

Cultivation: As it is tender and will not survive a winter outdoors, it should be treated as an annual, the seed being sown indoors in spring. Plant out in a warm sheltered position in May or put in window-boxes or pots that can then be conveniently placed on the kitchen window-sill or given the protection of a greenhouse. Planted beside tomatoes it will, appropriately, keep them disease free, but Culpeper firmly believed that if placed beside rue it would turn up its toes and die.

Harvest: Cut the leaves during summer and dry or freeze. The freezing method is recommended as much of the flavour is lost in the drying process.

BERGAMOT

Botanical name: Monarda didyma
Common name(s): Bee balm, Oswego tea, horsemint
Part(s) used: Leaves and flowers
Description: The brilliant red flowers of *Monarda didyma*, like small explosions of red bracts and florets, appear from late summer to mid-autumn

and are an adornment to any garden. They top the 2-3ft (60-90cm) high, square-shaped stems, the rough-surfaced ovate leaves growing in pairs up the length of the stem. So called because it has the delicious fragrance of bergamot oranges, there are numerous other varieties that have purple, lavender, pink and white flowers, though their foliage is seldom as fragrant. The red variety is named after Dr Nicholas Monardes, a Spanish doctor, botanist and writer, whose book *Joyful news out of the new founde world* appeared in the late sixteenth century.

Bergamot is a native of North America and the first plants, gathered apparently beside Lake Ontario, were introduced into this country in 1745. The leaves of the wild or purple bergamot, *M. fistulosa* were originally used to make a tea by the Indians who lived beside the Oswego River. The wild plant grew in great abundance in this area and was put to good use in 1773 following the Boston Tea Party. A stiff levy was placed on tea imported from the colonies, so the local tea rapidly gained in popularity and it is still drunk today.

To make Oswego tea, pour a cup of boiling water on one teaspoon of the dried leaves or three of the fresh.
A useful as well as a decorative plant in the garden, it attracts the bees and so aids pollination, hence its name bee balm. Its sweetly scented leaves and flowers can be used in salads and cool drinks though the flower heads are prone to harbour earwigs so soak well before using. It is not an important medicinal plant, but taken as an infusion it will relieve menstrual pain, vomiting and flatulence.

A favourite ingredient of fragrant articles, such as herb sleep pillows, or linen-cupboard sachets, the flowers and leaves are frequently used in pot-pourri, their bright colour and scent making them ideal components. The essential oil known as bergamot oil or bergamot orange is, in fact, extracted from the fruit *Citrus aurantium* and is popular with aromatherapists.

Pot-pourri
6oz (150g/2cups) of bergamot flowers and leaves
3oz (75g/1cup) of scented rose petals
3oz (75g/1cup) of scented geranium leaves

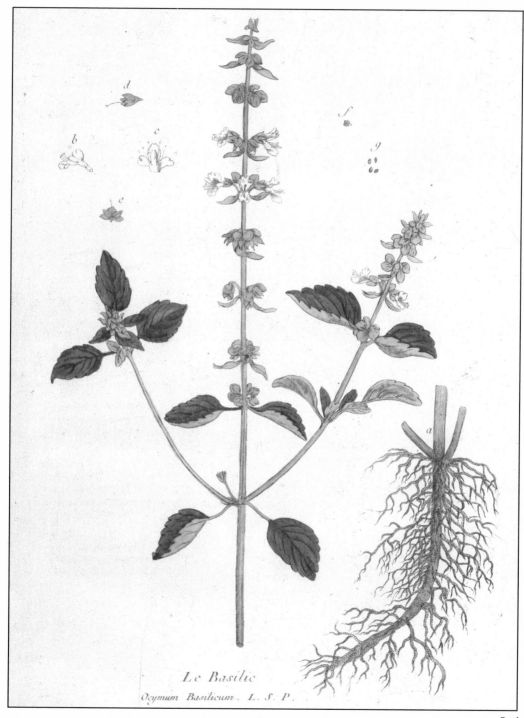

Le Basilic

Ocymum Basilicum. L. S. P.

Basil

Bergamot

3oz (75g/1cup) of lemon verbena leaves
3oz (75g/1cup) of dried lemon and orange peel
2tbs of salt
2tbs of orris root
1tsp of bergamot oil
3 drops of lemon grass oil

Cultivation: A perennial, it can be propagated by seed in spring or by dividing its creeping roots in spring or autumn. The centre of a clump of bergamot is apt to die back from the middle so division is recommended every other year, the outer parts being retained. It enjoys partial shade and a moist, light to medium soil.

Harvest: Gather the flowers and leaves during the summer and use fresh or dry.

BORAGE

Botanical name: Borago officinalis
Common name(s): Bugloss, burrage
Part(s) used: Flowers and leaves
Description: Growing to approximately 2ft (60cm) high borage has slightly drooping, brilliant blue, star-like flowers with black anthers. The hollow branched stems are rough and hairy, as are the leaves on both the upper and under sides. It is the delicious cool, cucumber flavour of these leaves that has made the herb so popular, along with its extraordinary ability to raise the spirits.

A native of southern Europe, borage has been grown in this country since medieval times and has become naturalized so efficiently that it is now a familiar sight on waste land. The Greeks and Romans appreciated a sprig of borage being added to their wine, Pliny commenting that it made men merry and joyful. He was not the only one over the centuries to extol its cheering effects; Gerard said 'Those of our time do use the flowers in sallads to exhilarate and make the mind glad. There be also many things made of these used everywhere for the comfort of the heart, for driving away of sorrow and increasing the joy of the mind.' The diarist John Evelyn agreed with him as did Francis Bacon who wrote that 'the leaf of Burrage hath an excellent spirit to repress the vapour of dusky melancholie'.

A pleasant addition to salads, both fruit and green, some find the leaves a tasty accompaniment to cheese and other savoury sandwiches and the fresh or crystallized flowers a decorative feature on cakes and puddings. They are certainly wildly attractive to bees and were considered pretty enough to be incorporated into pieces of early needlework. The ladies who were left to weep over their stitchery while their lords were away fighting in the Crusades certainly considered it a symbol of courage and gave it to their valiant knights as a stirrup cup.

Research has shown that it does have an effect on the adrenal gland and consequently the mental state of anyone who eats it. The scholars and herbalists in the past were right to extol its virtues. It has also been discovered that the seed contains a substance called gamma linolenic acid or GLA, an antidote to blood clotting, skin diseases and pre-menstrual stress. An infusion of borage leaves will not only raise the spirits but also reduces a fever and is said to stimulate the flow of a nursing mother's milk. A poultice can be made of the crushed leaves and used to relieve inflammation and reduce swelling.

Cultivation: A hardy annual, borage seed should be sown under glass in March and outdoors from April onwards. Once established it will self seed freely. A well-drained soil is recommended and a sunny position.

Harvest: If the leaves are to be dried pick them when they are young. Pick the flowers just before they are fully open and use fresh or dried, fortunately they retain their colour well when dried. The fresh leaves can be picked throughout the summer.

CARAWAY

Botanical name: Carum carvi
Common name(s): Caraway seed
Part(s) used: Roots and seeds
Description: Growing to 3ft (1m) or more high, caraway has the same delicate appearance of cow parsley. It boasts a long tap root that was a popular alternative to parsnips in the eighteenth century, feathery leaves and umbels of tiny white

flowers in May. A hardy biennial it flowers, then fruits (each small brown fruit containing two seeds) and dies in its second year. The very mention of caraway conjures up a picture of old maiden aunts enjoying a slice of seed cake but, in centuries past, it was much more widely used. There is evidence that it grew in the Mesolothic age in Europe, and it was certainly prescribed by early physicians as an antidote to flatulence. Due to it stimulating the digestive juices it will enliven a poor appetite and relieve a troublesome digestion. Simply chew a few seeds until the discomfort of wind or indigestion has passed. An infusion of the crushed seeds can also be taken to relieve indigestion and diarrhoea. Used as a gargle it will soothe an inflamed throat.

Always popular as a flavouring agent, a dish of caraway seeds on the dining table was a commonplace sight during the reign of Queen Elizabeth I; they were also a highly valued ingredient of old-fashioned love potions. Caraway is still used to flavour drinks such as Kummel and continues to be grown on a commercial scale in Germany and Holland. In America the seeds were given to children in church to prevent them hiccuping and they are still eaten as 'comfits' to sweeten the breath. These can be made by dipping the seeds in egg white after which they should be tossed in icing sugar and lemon juice and then left to harden.

The feathery leaves are a decorative and tasty addition to a salad and the roots can be cooked and eaten as a vegetable. The seeds will add a distinctive flavour to soups and stews, cream cheeses, breads and, of course, cakes. The following seed cake recipe is welcomingly and uncharacteristically moist, thanks to the inclusion of ground almonds. It is called a Sleightholmes cake and keeps well.

Sleightholmes cake
6oz (150g/2cups) butter
6oz (150g/2cups) caster sugar
3 eggs
1 level dessertspoonful/2tsp caraway seeds
1 level tablespoon/1tbs ground almonds
8oz (250g/2½cups) self-raising flour
Milk as needed

Cream the butter and sugar and stir in the caraway seeds. Separate the eggs and whisk the whites until stiff but not dry. Beat the yolks and fold carefully into the egg white. Add to the butter and sugar and stir in the ground almonds and flour, adding a little milk if the mixture seems stiff. Line a 2lb (900g) cake tin with greaseproof paper and pour in the mixture and level off. Bake in a moderate oven (350F/180C/Gas 4) for just over an hour. To test if it is cooked through, spear with a skewer. If it emerges clean, it is ready.

Cultivation: Propagate by seed only. Sow when the seed is ripe and fresh in the late summer or autumn to ensure flowers the following year. They should be sown where the plants are to flower, or the seedlings transplanted when they are small. Caraway likes well-drained soil and a sunny position.

Harvest: Remove the seed heads with care or they will be scattered and lost. Place a brown paper bag over the heads when the bunches are hung up to dry to ensure that all the seed is caught.

CHAMOMILE

Botanical name: Matricaria recutita (German chamomile); *Chamaemelum nobile* formerly *Anthemis nobilis* (Roman chamomile)
Part(s) used: Flowers and herb
Description: Christened 'Earth Apple' by the Greeks due to its scent being reminiscent of the fruit, chamomile was also considered a sacred herb by the Egyptians who dedicated it to their gods. Now frequently found growing wild on waste ground and favouring poor, sandy or gravel soil, it originated in western Europe and gradually spread and became naturalized. The foliage is feathery and retains its grey/green colour even in a drought. The flowers are daisy like, can be double, have white petals and dome-shaped yellow centres or receptacles. *Chamaemelum nobile* is compact and has creeping roots and a free-spreading habit, while *Matricaria recutita* is erect and has a more open habit.

Chamomile has many culinary, medicinal,

Caraway

cosmetic and other uses and should be considered an indispensable member of any collection of fresh or dried herbs. Once a popular strewing herb, it was a forerunner of the grass lawn as well as a sovereign remedy for sleeplessness. Parkinson wrote that 'Chamomile is put to divers and sundry uses, both for pleasure and profit, both for the sick and the sound, in bathing to comfort and strengthen the sound and to ease the pain of the diseased.' It is the more compact Roman chamomile that was used to scent herb seats in medieval gardens and is still used to make fragrant lawns. These can be rolled and mown just like a conventional turf lawn and positively thrive when walked upon, their only drawback being that they occasionally need weeding. When making a chamomile lawn it is best, if seed is sown, to raise the plants before transplanting them to the chosen site. This prevents the sward having a moth-eaten look due to patches of poor germination. The non-flowering variety 'Treneague' is another variety used in lawn making. It can be mixed with other herbs such as thyme but the gardener should be prepared for it to die down in winter.

Medicinally, it is the flowers that are of most value. The oil extracted from the plant has weak antiseptic and anti-inflammatory properties. This oil is a brilliant blue and more powerful if distilled before flowering; it is a yellow green and weaker if distilled after flowering. Half a dozen fresh flowers or a good teaspoon of the dried herb can be used to make an infusion that will act as a remedy for sleeplessness, irritability, rheumatic pain, nightmares and menstrual pain. It can be taken as a general tonic and used as a bathing herb that is effective in easing common aches and pains. One warning: drinking great quantities of this, once again popular, herbal tea can have a toxic effect. Only take it in moderation and if using the herb for medicinal purposes use the weaker double flowers rather than the stronger, single. Taken externally an infusion can also be used as a wash to soothe sore eyes or wiped on the skin as an insect repellent.

In the garden it will make a useful spray that will prevent the 'damping off' of seedlings and as a companion plant it is held in such high esteem

that it has earned the name 'plant's physician' for keeping its neighbours free of disease and pests. It certainly repels flying insects, bees included.

Perhaps one of its best known uses today is as an ingredient of a shampoo or rinse for blonde hair, to which it will add a brilliance, being a light bleach. To make this hair rinse make a strong infusion of fresh chamomile, 6oz (150g/2cups) of the herb to 1pt (600ml/2½cups) of water. Infuse for at least twenty minutes and use before it cools.

Cultivation: Propagate German chamomile, which is a hardy annual, by seed and plant out in the sun, in poor, well-drained soil. Roman chamomile is a hardy perennial and can be grown in seed trays in early spring and then transplanted, or propagated by cuttings taken from side shoots in the summer.

Harvest: Gather the flowers when they are at their best and use fresh or dry and store.

CHERVIL

Botanical name: Anthriscus cerefolium
Common name(s): Mirris
Part(s) used: Leaves
Description: A member of the carrot family, chervil grows up to 18in (45cm) high and has fern-like foliage similar to that of cow parsley though when grown in bright sunlight, it is tinged with pink. It bears umbels of tiny flowers on ribbed and hollow stems which go on to produce beak-shaped seeds. Resist the temptation of gathering it from the wild as it can easily be mistaken for a toxic plant of similar appearance such as hemlock.

A native of south-eastern Europe and Asia Minor it was introduced to this country by the Romans who planted it near their camps. It has been cultivated ever since, escaping from the garden and becoming naturalized in the wild, though it was more widely used in the fifteenth, sixteenth and seventeenth centuries than it is today.

More a culinary than a medicinal herb it is more commonly used in France and is an essential ingredient of *fines herbes* along with tarragon and parsley. A strong aromatic plant, its flavour is similar to that of parsley though there is a welcome hint of fennel, which is warming and pleasing. Chervil associates wonderfully with egg and fish dishes and can also be made into a useful savoury butter.

Chervil with turbot

Take a whole turbot, one that will fit into the frying pan, and place it in the pan in which 2-3oz (50g/4tbs-75g/1cup) of butter has been melted. Cook gently on both sides for about five minutes and then pour over a ¼pt-½pt (140ml/½cup-280ml/1¼cups) of single cream, depending on the size of the fish. Let it simmer and then add a large handful of chopped chervil, salt and pepper to taste, and serve. The delicate flavour of the fish is brought out by the herb, rather than being swamped or spoiled by it, and the flecks of green form an attractive contrast to the white flesh of the turbot and the cream.

As a medicinal herb its effects are toning and cleansing. It is a diuretic, thought to be a brain stimulant, will improve a flagging memory, lift the spirits and calm the nerves. An infusion can be taken to lower the blood pressure and a poultice of the crushed leaves used to relieve haemorrhoids and rheumatic pain.

Cultivation: Sow fresh seed *in situ* in the autumn to ensure an early crop of leaves, or in spring at three-week intervals. To ensure a constant crop it can also be grown in trays in the greenhouse during the winter. It germinates quickly and runs to seed so it is best not transplanted as this provokes the plants to flower. It grows best in a cool, damp and shady spot.

Harvest: Pick the leaves for drying before the plant flowers or blanch small bunches of fresh leaves and freeze.

CHIVES

Botanical name: Allium schoenoprasum
Alternative common name(s): Cives, civet, sweth, rush leeks
Part(s) used: Herb
Description: A member of the vast onion family

that embraces the leek as well as garlic, this perennial is one of the most widely grown and familiar of herbs. The small elongated bulbs grow in clusters and throw up a large head of tubular, blue-green, grass-like leaves. These grow to between 5-10in (12.5-25cm) high and in June and July produce pinky-mauve flowers similar to thrift. If grown for culinary purposes these pretty flower heads, that stand slightly higher than the 'grass', should be cut so as to promote growth and ensure that the foliage remains tender.

Always accommodating, if allowed to flower, chives will make a charming edging plant in the kitchen and ornamental garden and will also act as an effective 'doctor'. A useful as well as an attractive companion plant it will keep fruit trees free of scab at the same time as forming a delightful ring of colour at their base. It is frequently used to protect roses against black spot and aphids and if planted alongside carrots will frighten off the greedy carrot fly. It is also an ideal candidate for the pot or window-box close to hand outside the kitchen door or window as it has surprisingly fast regenerative powers when cut and good manners, spreading only slowly and modestly.

A native of temperate northern Europe, it might well have been introduced by the Romans, but was not cultivated in this country until the Middle Ages. It was listed by Emperor Charlemagne in his *Capitulare de Vilis* written in 812 and was also well known to Gerard and Culpeper. The Victorian gardener-writer, John Loudon, wrote of it that 'No cottage garden ought to be without chives: it forms one of the most wholesome herbs for chopping and mixing among the food for young chickens, ducks and turkeys – making them thrive wonderfully, and preventing that pest the gripes'. Chives have no medicinal uses though eaten regularly they will stimulate the appetite and help combat anaemia.

This plant is highly recommended for its culinary uses, and whether eaten raw or heated (it should not be cooked but added late to hot dishes), it leaves little smell on the breath. A classic addition to omelettes, potato salad, yoghurt and cream cheeses, it makes a tasty herb butter, salad garnish and flavouring for soups.

The following very simple recipe has a delicate and subtle flavour that is, at first, hard to identify, but unfailingly enjoyed by all, whether served hot or cold.

Avocado and chive soup
2 avocados
2 tbs of chopped chives
1pt (600 ml/2½ cups) of chicken stock
¼pt (140 ml/½ cup) of single cream
¼pt (140 ml/½ cup) of plain yoghurt
1 tsp of sugar

Blend half the chicken stock, the avocados, yoghurt and cream together. Place in a saucepan with the chives and remaining stock. Heat and serve garnished with fresh chives.

Cultivation: The clump of bulbs should be divided in spring or autumn or seed sown in trays indoors, or outside in drills in spring. Chives are greedy feeders so the soil should be well fed especially in pots or window-boxes. Seek out a variety called 'garlic' chives, flavoured as might be expected.

Harvest: The 'grass' can be cut throughout the year but if a constant fresh supply is not available, it is best cut in the summer and frozen rather than dried. The foliage takes a long time to dry so much of the flavour is lost during the drying process.

COMFREY

Botanical name: Symphytum officinale
Alternative common name(s): Knitbone, knitback, boneset, bruisewort, church bells
Part(s) used: Leaves and root
Description: This member of the borage family was an important bone-setting herb in the Middle Ages, hence its country and Latin name, the Greek word *sympho* meaning 'to make whole'. A native to most of Europe, from Scandinavia to Turkey, it is thought to have been introduced to this country by the returning Crusader knights and was consequently given the name of 'Saracen's Root'. A perennial, it favours wet ground and can frequently be seen growing beside pools and streams and in damp meadows.

Growing 2-3ft (60-90cm) high, the hollow stem and ovate leaves are covered with short stiff hairs, the foliage decreasing in size as it advances up the stem. The creamy-white or pink-mauve bell-shaped flowers that grow in pairs appear in early summer and autumn and dangle characteristically in a row to one side of the top of the plant.

At thirty-five per cent comfrey has a surprisingly high protein content, which puts it on a par with the soya bean; it also contains B12 which is rarely found in edible plants. Although it has been used as an animal feed, especially to pigs, and is a favourite with cattle and horses (it was once thought that it cured and warded off foot and mouth disease), full advantage has never been taken of its protein and vitamin content.

The same cannot be said of the medicinal qualities of what is considered one of the best known of all the healing plants. An astringent as well as an antiseptic, its healing and soothing qualities are particularly well suited to the treatment of sprains and breaks. Gerard said of it that the 'slimie substance of the roots made in a posset of ale, be given to cure pains in the back suffered by wrestlers and immoderate wenchers' and Culpeper wrote that it was 'special good for ruptures and broken bones'.

The plants contains allantoin and mucilage (a substance that forms a gel when mixed with water) which promotes the reconnecting of tissue. A mash of the leaves or root can be made into a warm poultice that will reduce inflammation and swelling and so expedite the healing of the affected part. Such a poultice will also treat bruises and draw the poison from boils. A decoction of the root, ½oz (14g) to 1½pt (840ml/3¾ cups) of water or milk and simmered for fifteen minutes and taken in small doses, is an old-fashioned remedy for bronchial and pulmonary ailments. An infusion of the fresh or dried leaves will clear the skin, relieve sinus trouble and purify the blood. Mixed with other herbs, sweetened with honey and flavoured with lemon, comfrey makes a pleasant and beneficial tea. But do not take to excess, or even on a daily basis, because it can cause liver damage due to the presence of pyrrolizidine alkaloids. Those suffer-

Comfrey and daisy

ing from aching joints would also do well to use it in a healing herbal bath. Place the fresh leaves in a muslin bag and hang it beneath the running tap. This will help relax the muscles and soothe aching joints.

If comfrey's medicinal qualities were not sufficient reason to include this versatile herb in the garden, the fresh leaf is also a good composting plant. Cut and laid in the bottom of a trench dug for potatoes it will increase the crop and keep them free of scab. Left to soak in water, the leaves will also make an economical liquid manure. The enthusiastic and inventive cook should not pass it by for the fresh leaves can be chopped and used in salads, or cooked like spinach – it is very nutritious.

Cultivation: Take care where you plant comfrey as it is hard to eradicate once established and is best placed in a corner of the garden. It likes a moist, fertile soil, and a shady position. Divide the roots in autumn or take root cuttings in the spring or autumn.

Harvest: Gather the leaves for drying in summer and the roots in autumn.

CAUTION: Comfrey contains a constituent alkaloid which is known to be toxic. Avoid taking this herb internally on a regular basis as experiments using the isolated alkaloid have shown it to be damaging to the liver. There has not been any evidence of the whole herb causing similar damage. Contact a qualified herbalist for advice.

There are no restrictions on using comfrey externally – it is totally safe when applied to the skin.

CORIANDER

Botanical name: Coriandrum sativum
Common name(s): Chinese parsley, cilantro, dizzycorn, Japanese parsley
Part(s) used: Leaves, seeds
Description: The interest now taken in Indian cookery has happily brought about the widespread availability of fresh coriander, though a word of warning will not go amiss: if you are not familiar with the plant always check that it is a bunch of coriander you are buying as the foliage can easily be mistaken for the large-leafed parsley. An annual and member of the carrot family, it has glossy bi-pinnate leaves with finely dissected edges, and flat umbels of pale lilac flowers in July and August. The whole plant smells rancid and unpleasant when young, but when ripe and ready to harvest, the round seeds have a pungent, honey and citrus scent that is quite pleasant.

Cultivated for thousands of years, coriander was most probably brought to Britain by the Romans. It was obviously grown widely in Tudor times for it was an ingredient of a drink served at weddings called Hippocras. It was thought to be an aphrodisiac and consumed excessively is known to act as a narcotic.

An infusion of the crushed seeds combats flatulence and prevents griping caused by certain remedies such as laxatives, so they are a useful ingredient of senna tea. Chewing the seeds will stimulate the gastric juices and Arab women are known to use it to ease their labour pains. An increasingly popular culinary herb, it associates deliciously with lamb, chicken, ham, pork and smoked meats; it is a staple ingredient of curries and in seed or leaf form can be used to garnish a salad or, with a dash of lemon, add a delicious flavour to stuffings. The leaves should always be used fresh and not dried. The following recipe produces juices that are creamy and full of the faintly peppery exotic after-taste of coriander.

Coriander chicken
1½lb (675g) of boneless chicken
1 large cooking apple peeled and cut into chunks
2 large carrots chopped into rounds
1 large onion peeled and sliced
½lb (112g) of mushrooms sliced
3tbs (heaped) of flour
1pt (600ml/2½cups) of dry cider
2tbs of chopped fresh coriander
3tsp of mild French mustard
¼ (140ml/½cup) of soured cream

Heat oven to Gas 4 (350F/180C) and melt a little oil and 2oz (50g/4tbs) of butter in a fireproof casserole. Cut the chicken into small pieces and place in the casserole with chopped onions and carrots. Stir in the flour, add the cider and stir. Add seasoning, coriander and mustard. Bring to the boil and when it thickens transfer to the centre of the oven and leave for three quarters of an hour. Stir once or twice during that time. After three quarters of an hour add chopped apple and mushrooms and return to the oven for a further twenty minutes. Stir in sour cream and garnish with fresh coriander before serving.

Cultivation: Coriander likes a sunny, sheltered position and fairly heavy, fertile soil. Sow the seed indoors in spring and outdoors in drills during early summer and then thin. It makes an attractive mid-border plant.

Harvest: The leaves can be picked at any time, the seeds at the end of the summer. Their scent improves with age.

DANDELION

Botanical name: Taraxacum officinale
Common name(s): Pis en lit, piss a bed, pee in the bed, lion's teeth, fairy clock
Part(s) used: All parts of the plant
Description: The French called it '*dents de lion*' as the drawings in old herbals depicted the leaves as jagged as a lion's teeth, hence its name today. The edges of its long leaves that grow from the base of the plant certainly have a fearsome, tooth-like appearance. Though it is flat faced, it is the golden flowers borne on hollow leafless stems, that most catch the eye. It is, perhaps wrongly, the most despised of all weeds due to the ease with which it seeds and makes itself at home almost anywhere, from meadows to pavements. But if seen for the very first time, without any preconceptions, few could fail not to be charmed by both its brilliant, sun-like flowers and delicate fruit or 'clock' of gossamer seed heads.

A much valued medicinal herb due to the fact that all parts of the plant can be used with safety and in large amounts, it is an effective diuretic (as its common names might imply) and laxative. An infusion of the leaves and root will help the liver, gallbladder and kidneys to function normally, aid digestion and stimulate the appetite.

Dandelion tea, or fresh leaves eaten regularly, will purify the blood and improve the complexion, and the white juice which flows when the plant is cut can be dabbed on warts or spots, though do not be surprised when they turn black before disappearing.

Some will remember dandelion coffee being made from the chopped and roasted root when conventional coffee was not available during the war, and should not rule it out as a beverage today. It is a sleep-inducing rather than reducing drink and will benefit those suffering from rheumatism and indigestion. The tender young leaves (avoid the old bitter ones) are full of vitamins and minerals, even copper and iron. Used regularly in salads they can be eaten to combat anaemia and will help clear skin complaints.

The roots and leaves can be made into a decoction and the leaves into a mild infusion. The following recipe is for a dry, sherry-type wine, that makes a generally beneficial, as well as pleasant drink.

Dandelion wine
3pt (1½l/7½cups) of flower heads
8pt (4½l/20cups) of boiling water
2 oranges
1 lemon
3lb (1350g) of sugar
1oz (28g/2tbs) of yeast

Place the flower heads in a large bowl and cover with all the boiling water. Leave for several days, stirring daily. Place in a preserving pan and add the pithless rind of two large oranges and one of lemon, bring to the boil and simmer. Remove from the heat and add the sugar and when lukewarm strain through muslin and add the juice of the oranges and lemon and stir in the yeast. Leave for a few days and then strain, through muslin again, into bottles. Cork loosely for several weeks until fermentation has ceased and resist from drinking for at least six months.

Cultivation: It is more a matter of controlling the spread of dandelions. They can be grown from seed sown deep in drills in April or from small pieces of root. Dandelions belong to the rare

Dandelion

parthenogenetic group of plants which produce seed that has no need to be fertilized by an outside agent. Popular with bees, they flower early in the year, but should be cut if the leaves are to be harvested.

Harvest: Gather the leaves and flowers in spring, summer and autumn and the roots in autumn.

DILL

Botanical name: Anethum graveolens
Part(s) used: Leaves, flowers and seeds
Description: A half-hardy annual that resembles fennel in that it has feathery leaves and umbels of small yellow flowers, dill has been used as a culinary and medicinal herb from the beginning of civilization. John Josselyn, who travelled in New England in the seventeenth century, mentions how well it grew in North America once it had been introduced even though it originally came from the Mediterranean region of Europe.

The leaves and seeds are used to flavour food, fish and pickles in particular, while only the seeds are used medicinally. Its name comes from the old Norse word, *dilla*, which means to lull and being an important ingredient of gripe water, it is still used to soothe fractious babies. It is a remedy for flatulence and indigestion and Culpeper recommended that a decoction be made of the bruised seed or herb which, if drunk with white wine, 'is a gallant expeller of wind and provoker of terms'. Used by medieval witches in their love and other potions it was also hung in a dwelling to ward off the 'evil eye'

Malt vinegar in which dill seeds have been left to soak for a few days is popular and, as John Parkinson wrote in 1629, when 'put among pickled cucumbers … it doth very well agree'. Its delicate anise flavour deserves to be made more of in this country where it is still seldom used, those living in Scandinavia and eastern European countries valueing it much more highly. Try chopping and sprinkling it over new potatoes or even peas in place of parsley or mint. Dill salad with kipper fillets makes a colourful and fresh-tasting starter in which the raw fillets of fish are 'cooked' by the tasty vinaigrette.

Kipper fillets and dill salad
8 kipper fillets
½lb (225g) of eating apples
6oz (150g/2cups) of cooked beetroot
1 small onion
6tbs of olive oil
1½tbs of wine vinegar
1tsp of French mustard
1tsp of sugar
1tbs (heaped) of fresh dill
Salt and pepper

Cut the kipper fillets into thin strips and dice the apples, beetroot and onion and place in separate bowls. Make a dressing of the olive oil, wine vinegar, French mustard, sugar, salt and pepper and chopped dill weed. A few hours before serving add the dressing to the separate bowls mixing them altogether just before serving.

Cultivation: Dill should be grown from seed only, in April outside and March inside. It takes about two weeks to germinate, though it is not always easy to get it to flourish. A good 12in (30cm) should be left in between each plant. It likes a rich soil and a sunny, but sheltered position. The seed stays viable for several years.

Harvest: Gather the leaves before the plant comes into flower or after the seed has set. It is best used fresh. The seeds can be used fresh or dried and should be gathered in late summer and autumn.

ELDER

Botanical name: Sambucus nigra
Alternative common name(s): Black elder, bore tree, bour tree, common elder, pipe tree
Part(s) used: Leaves, flowers, bark and berries
Description: Called the 'medicine chest of the country people' almost every part of this shrub can be put to good use. Growing to approximately 20ft (6m) high the shrub or small tree bears flat clusters of creamy white flowers in June that are followed by shiny black berries in autumn. The flowers give off a strong scent of Muscat grapes, though the smell of the leaves when crushed is far from pleasant. Happily, they can be put to good use in the garden as they act

Dill

Elder

as an insecticide and protect fruit and vegetables from being damaged by aphids and greenfly.

Elder was a traditional addition to most herb gardens in times past, when all the herbs in the garden were under the protection of the Elder Mother or Spirit of the Elder. It was believed that if you stood underneath it at midnight on midsummer night you would see the King of the Elves go by and if you planted one near the house it would guard the inhabitants from the evil spells of witchcraft and thunder. The Greeks and Romans used the hard wood to make musical instruments and Pliny noted that the most melodic of pan pipes were made of Elder. Certain habits remain constant over the centuries and the straight branches, when the pith has been

extracted, are still made into pea-shooters just as Culpeper mentioned in his herbal: 'every boy that plays with a potgun will not mistake another tree instead of the elder'.

Elder is a most versatile herb, and its culinary, medicinal and cosmetic uses are legion. A small bunch of flowers tied up in muslin and cooked along with the fruit adds a delicate flavour to gooseberry fool and ice cream, and the syrup is a delicious addition to a fruit salad. The bunches of small purple-black berries with which the Romans dyed their hair, give a dark, rich colour to wines, jams and jellies and add a colourful dash of interest to pies and crumbles. But take note, these shiny little berries should not be eaten raw. Very little can beat the pleasure of drinking a

Elderberries

glass of chilled elderberry champagne or cordial on a summer's evening. It is easy to make and always popular.

Elderflower cordial
24-32 large elderflower heads (early blooms are best for, if picked late, they are apt to ferment the mixture
4 lemons
2oz (50g/4tbs) of citric acid
4lbs (1800g) of plain white sugar

Cut off all the flowers and disgard all the green stalks. Put the flowers, sliced lemon, citric acid and sugar into a big plastic bowl or bucket and add a kettleful of boiling water. Stir until all the sugar has dissolved, then cover the bowl with cling film (plastic film), leaving the handle of the wooden spoon sticking out. The mixture needs stirring 3-4 times daily without removing the spoon from the bucket. Continue for 4-5 days, then strain the liquid into bottles. It can be served with soda or clear water, vodka but not gin.

As a medicinal herb an infusion of elder flowers can be taken to treat flu and colds and clear the upper respiratory system, while the berries can be made into a soothing syrup or jam which will act as a gentle laxative. The leaves are used as a green dye and the green bark, underlying the top layer of the grey bark, can be made into a decoction that is an effective diuretic and laxative. Elder flowers have considerable soothing and healing powers and an infusion used externally will whiten and soften the skin and act as an astringent for an oily skin.

Cultivation: Elder will grow anywhere but favours moist soil. Take hardwood cuttings in the autumn and winter and plant outside, and soft stem cuttings in the spring. It can be grown from seed outdoors in spring but the bushes will take about five years to bear flowers.

Harvest: The flowers should be gathered for drying just before they open and, if used fresh, before they become overblown. The berries should be picked when they are ripe.

ELECAMPANE

Botanical name: Inula helenium
Alternative common name(s): Elf dock, horseheal, scabwort, velvet dock, wild sunflower
Part(s) used: Root
Description: Now seldom seen in the wild, this tall, (it grows to 5ft (1.5m)), stately perennial that originated in central Asia, relishes a damp and shady position. It has a striking, architectural shape – vast 18in (45cm) leaves that are downy beneath and smooth on top, strong stem and golden sunflower-like flowers – that add a touch of drama to a border and justifies its more widespread use in the ornamental garden. There are not many plants that are so bold in appearance and it is surprising that it is not more popular for it is an ideal candidate for the back of a border and an eye-catching feature in a moist, shaded bed. Few summer-flowering perennials will tolerate such conditions.

A medicinal rather than a culinary herb (though it has been used to flavour bitter liqueurs such as Absinthe), the exceptionally large root is the most valued part of the herb. It should be gathered before it is allowed to get tough and woody. When cut, dried and crushed this turns from white to grey, smells of violets and can be made into a fragrant infusion or a decoction. This can be used to treat bronchial problems or a bad digestion. In the past it was used to treat consumption and considered an effective remedy for whooping cough. Culpeper firmly believed that it 'stays the spreading of the venom of serpents, as also putrid and pestilential fevers, and the plague itself'. Elecampane is usually used in conjunction with another herb that has similar medicinal properties and a decoction can be made by placing 1oz (28g/2tbs) of root in a pan of cold water that, covered with a lid, is brought to the boil and then left to cool. This can be used externally to treat skin conditions or taken in wine-glass doses.

Known and written about by the Greeks and Romans, the root was originally boiled and eaten as a palatable vegetable that promoted good digestion as well as mirth. Popular in the Middle Ages, it was later sliced and eaten as an appetizer, candied, or made into lozenges to treat asthmatic

Elecampane

conditions. The settlers took it to America where it gained a good reputation as a remedy for skin problems and horse and sheep medicine, hence its common name, horseheal. There are several tales as to how it acquired its Latin name. One tells that Helen, the wife of Menelaus, plucked it as she was being abducted by Paris, another is that it sprang from her tears. *Enula campana* was its original name at a time when it grew in the fields around Rome, in the country or *compagna*. A more prosaic and believable explanation, but one that lacks romance, is that it grew particularly well on the island of St Helena.

Cultivation: Propagate by dividing the roots in the autumn or sowing the seeds in the spring. It likes a moist soil and semi shade, will self seed and should always be put to the back of a border.

Harvest: Gather the roots in the autumn.

EVENING PRIMROSE

Botanical name: Oenothera biennis
Alternative common name(s): Tree primrose
Part(s) used: Leaves, stalk, root and seeds
Description: So much has recently been discovered about the medicinal virtues of this striking flowering biennial that its name has now become one of the most talked about of all healing herbs. Growing up to 4ft (1.2m) high in its second year (it produces only a rosette of leaves in its first) the plant bears cup-shaped yellow flowers that only open between six and seven in the evening. Composed of only four petals, these have a delicate smell and appear during the summer and early autumn.

The leaves are borne on branching reddish stems, are alternate and about 1½in (4cm) in length. A native of North and South America it was introduced to the British Isles via the botanic garden in Padua at the beginning of the seventeenth century and can now be seen growing wild throughout the country.

Up until a decade ago the leaves and outer skin of the stalk were the only part of the herb to be used, apart from the root that can be eaten as a vegetable. As a sedative, astringent and demulcent they were a remedy for asthma, whooping cough and stomach upsets. Today it is the oil that is extracted from the seeds that makes the evening primrose one of the most valuable of all the medicinal herbs.

Original research carried out in 1981 proved that it greatly alleviated the ill effects of premenstrual syndrome and the menopause. It will soothe the hyperactive, is a treatment for eczema as well as being a prescribed treatment for those suffering from the after-effects of alcoholic poisoning.

Consequent research has also shown that it can prevent the blood clotting and will relieve the pain of arthritis and rheumatism. The herb contains fatty acids such as gamma linolenic acid or GLA, that triggers the regeneration of cells, and has even been used with some success to combat multiple sclerosis. All those who have benefited from evening primrose will agree that it is a king among medicinal herbs. It not only offers relief from painful complaints but protects against the often more harmful side-effects of various chemical drugs.

Health food shops and chemists now stock evening primrose, either as a medicinal remedy or as a natural beauty aid. The oil can be used externally and internally, and will help moisturize the skin and improve the condition of the hair.

It is an attractive plant in the herb and ornamental garden and there are several different varieties. *Oenothera acaulis* has attractive white flowers that fade to pink, and *Oenothera sulphurea* and *Oenothera tetragona* 'Sundrops' have reddish toothed leaves and flowers that fade to a delicate pale and striking, dark apricot.

Cultivation: Evening primrose will grow on any well-drained soil and will tolerate some shade. It seeds itself freely but can also be propagated by root division or offsets. Seed should be sown as soon as it is ripe in the autumn.

Harvest: Gather the leaves, flowers and seeds in summer and the root in early autumn when it is still young. The seed from which the oil is extracted commercially is gathered when ripe.

FENNEL

Botanical name: Foeniculum vulgare
Alternative common name(s): Fenkel, wild fennel,
sweet fennel
Part(s) used: Leaves, root and seed
Description: Now a classic accompaniment to oily
fish such as mackerel, fennel has been used as a
medicinal herb since ancient times. A perennial,
it can grow to over 6ft (1.8m) tall, has stout
stalks, blue-green feathery foliage (its name is
derived from the latin word for hay, *foenum*), and
large umbels of yellow flowers. The fact that it is
a mild diuretic most probably led the ancient
Greeks to think of it as an effective slimming
agent, though what led them and later genera-
tions to think it gave courage and prolonged life,
is less obvious. Certainly the Greek athletes
consumed it in the hope that it would improve
their performance and strength, and later the old
herbalists recommended it as a remedy for a poor
memory.

In the Middle Ages it was eaten to relieve the
pangs of hunger and Culpeper states in his herbal
that the 'seed boiled in wine and drunk, is good
for those that are biten with serpents, or have eat
poisonfull herbs or mushrooms' and that it would
'help shortness of breath and wheezing'. Fennel
tea which can be made with the leaves or crushed
seeds will calm indigestion, prevent flatulence,
clear the bronchial tubes, soothe bad coughs,
whooping cough and asthma. The tea made with
1oz (28g/2tbs) of the herb to 1pt (600ml/
2½cups) of boiling water, and drunk before each
meal, can also be taken by those wishing to lose
weight. Of particular use to women, it can be
taken to alleviate menstrual pain, is said to
increase the flow of milk and, used as a poultice
will heal painful, swollen breasts.

The flavour of fennel is like that of aniseed
mixed with parsley, and the fragrance sweet. The
bulb-like lower bowl of Florence fennel Finoc-
chio, *Foeniculum dulce* can be eaten as a
vegetable, either raw to add a warm spicy flavour
to salads or steamed, braised or boiled like celery.
The chopped fresh or dried leaves are an
attractive and tasty garnish for fish such as
salmon and mackerel, and will add a pleasant zest
to a salad. The seeds can be used in bread and
cakes though fennel being one of the strongest
herbs, should always be used with discretion so as
not to overwhelm all other flavours. A different,
simple to make and flavoursome sauce for rather
bland white fish can be made from Florentine
fennel.

Fennel and leek sauce
1 bulb of Florentine fennel
3 tender young leeks
2oz (50g/4tbs) of butter
⅛pt (75ml) of single cream
Salt and pepper
1tsp of fresh or dried fennel leaves
Pinch of sugar

Lightly cook the leeks in the butter and boil the
fennel. Blend and sieve, then add the cream,
chopped fennel leaves and season with salt and
pepper. A pinch of sugar always serves to bring
out the flavour, add as desired.

Bronze fennel, *F. officinale nigra*, is an attractive
plant to have in the ornamental garden, the soft
reddish haze of foliage forming an ideal foil to
apricot and red-flowering plants or those with
bolder foliage.

Cultivation: Fennel likes a well-drained, sheltered but sunny position and though a perennial
should be replanted every three years to ensure a
strong, healthy plant. Propagate by dividing or
sowing seed outdoors in the spring or autumn.
Bronze fennel should be treated in the same way
but Florence fennel is an annual and should have
its flowers removed.

Harvest: Gather the leaves for drying or freezing
in early summer before the flowers appear and
collect the seeds in September.

FEVERFEW

Botanical name: Tanacetum parthenium formerly
Chrysanthemum parthenium
Alternative common name(s): Batchelor's buttons,
featherfew, featherfoil, flirtwort, maydes' weed
Part(s) used: Herb
Description: A native of Yugoslavia, feverfew is
one of those plants that the gardener is happy to
allow to seed itself freely, especially the golden

COLEOPTERA . Coccinella .

Fennel

leaved 'Aureum'. This has yellowy rather than fresh green, frilly edged leaves and flat-topped clusters of pretty, white, daisy-like flowers, the whole resembling a miniature 1-2ft (30-60cm) chrysanthemum. Frequently seen growing in hedgerows or from cracks in walls, this bitter-scented herb was commonly used to treat 'agues' and the name feverfew is derived from the Latin word *febrifugia*, a substance that allays fevers. Culpeper wrote of it that:

It is very effectual for all pains in the head coming of a cold cause, the herb being bruised and applied to the crown of the head: as also for a vertigo, that is, a turning or swimming in the head. The decoction thereof drunk warm, and the herb bruised with a few corns of bay-salt, and applied to the wrists before the coming of the ague fits, does take them away.

Modern research has revealed its impressive ability to prevent migraine. If several leaves are eaten daily a high percentage of sufferers will enjoy complete or partial relief from those incapacitating headaches. But a word of warning here to those who have never tried this remedy: eating feverfew can cause mouth ulcers. The patient must be on the look out for this unwelcome side-effect and weigh the benefits against the disadvantages or, as is now possible, take feverfew in tablet form. An infusion of the dried leaves taken in wine-glass doses as a tonic is a remedy for poor digestion and also eases and provokes menstruation, feverfew has always been considered a herb of special use to women. It will also act as a mild sedative.

The scent of the plant, which has been likened to stale chamomile, has its uses. It effectively repels bugs such as mosquitoes, gnats, moths and bees; its insecticidal properties are similar to those of *pyrethrum*. When sitting out in the garden on a summer's evening, wipe any exposed parts of the body with an infusion of the leaves and flowers and you will be left well alone.

Cultivation: Feverfew enjoys a well-drained sunny position. It can be grown from root division, stem cuttings taken in spring or from seed. The seed should be sown indoors in March or outdoors in April, though it self seeds freely.

Harvest: Gather the leaves in midsummer. They can be dried or frozen.

FOXGLOVE

Botanical name: Digitalis purpurea
Alternative common name(s): Witches' gloves, dead men's bells, fairy's glove, gloves of Our Lady, bloody fingers, virgin's glove, fairy caps, folk's glove, fairy thimbles
Part(s) used: Leaves
Description: The statuesque beauty of this native plant makes it popular in both the herb and ornamental garden. Wonderfully adaptable, it looks as much at home in a cultivated plot as it does growing in the wild. It can grow to about 5ft(1.5m) tall, is a biennial and bears its tubular, bell-like, purple flowers from June to August. It was these that gave the plant its common name, as they resemble the fingers of gloves that were thought to have belonged to the 'good folk' or fairies.

In 1542 the German herbalist Leonhard Fuchs named it *Digitalis, digitabulum* being the Latin word for thimble. Mentioned by Gerard, Parkinson and Culpeper in their herbals, the crushed leaves were used as a poultice to heal wounds or, in the form of a decoction, were a remedy for a 'scabby head' or taken to 'purge the body both upwards and downwards'.

The foxglove is what could be called a milestone plant on the evolutionary road of scientific medicine. In 1785 an English doctor, William Withering, discovered that when using foxglove leaves to treat dropsy it was actually the heart that was most affected. Having been stimulated it triggered off reactions in other parts of the body, such as the kidneys, provoking them to clear the fluid which had caused the dropsy. When he analysed the tea made with dried foxglove leaves, a local Shropshire recipe, it was found that they contained glycosides such as digitalin which has a dramatic effect on the muscles of the heart.

Withering wrote a thesis on his research on digitalin, describing many case histories and was

Foxgloves and male fern

rewarded for his efforts by being made a Fellow of the Royal Society. He died in 1799, his work completed, and a memorial suitably depicting a foxglove was placed in Edgbaston Old Church. In such a way did the herb come to be used to treat heart failure, its valuable ingredients being extracted and refined to produce a drug that is commonly used today. Medical herbalists do not use *Digitalis* to treat heart failure but another plant with a less toxic action. A verbal skull and crossbones should be added here as under no circumstances should the foxglove be used in home-made preparations of any kind. **All parts are poisonous.**

Digitalis purpurea is the true herb, but there are some delightful garden varieties such as *D. lanata* with its pearl and purple old-fashioned coal scuttle-shaped flowers and *D. lutea* that has small lemon blooms and *D. grandiflora* that has large sulphur bells. The pure white flowers of *D. purpurea* 'Alba' always look charming either to the back of a border or in the informal or woodland garden. All are attractive to bees.

Cultivation: The foxglove freely seeds itself, enjoys partial shade and a light, acid soil, though it is tolerant of a wide variety of situations. Sow seeds in the spring out of doors or in trays and plant out in the chosen flowering position in September. It will frequently flower for two years before dying.

Harvest: Gather the seed in late summer when it has ripened for planting the following year. Do not use foxgloves as a home remedy – they are too dangerous.

GARLIC

Botanical name: Allium sativum
Alternative common name(s): Poor man's treacle
Part(s) used: Bulb
Description: So worthy of its status and for so long, both as a culinary and a medicinal herb, we have long since lost track of the provenance of this inestimable herb. As ancient as the oldest civilizations, there is sound evidence that it was fed to the slaves that built the pyramids and it also features in Chinese mythology as a means to

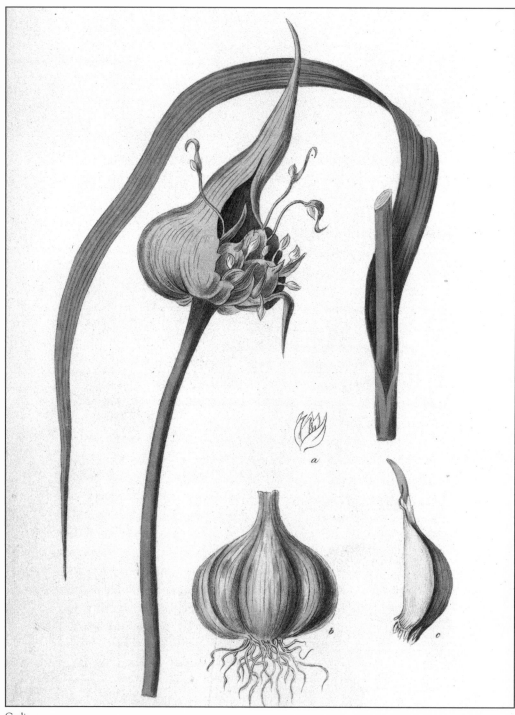

Garlic

ward off the evil eye. It was later prescribed to the athletes competing at the original Olympic games as a protection against the plague and to ensure they were not troubled by insect bites.

Garlic is rich in potassium and vitamin C and it is well known that eaten regularly it will ward off coughs and colds and clear the bronchial tubes most effectively. Many still consider that simply to carry a clove somewhere on one's person is as beneficial as actually eating it. Garlic is used as a preventative against angina and arteriosclerosis and is also taken to reduce blood cholesterol. Once crushed and exposed to the air, it has a strong antibacterial action and during the First World War, when many chemical drugs were not available, garlic was applied to wounds to prevent them from turning gangrenous. It can also protect the digestive system from harmful bacteria and is an excellent natural remedy for dysentry and diarrhoea as well as an effective treatment for worms.

There is only one disadvantage to eating this versatile herb and that is the smell it leaves lingering, treacherously, on the breath. Thankfully, help is at hand in the form of parsley or coffee beans. Munch either one after eating raw or cooked garlic and no friends will be lost.

The following recipe makes a delicious, and economical, starter to any meal. Mushrooms grilled under a pat of the garlic butter commonly associated with snails, create a pungent, crunchy and juicy dish.

Garlic mushrooms
6oz (150g/2cups) of butter
2 cloves of garlic
1oz (28g/2tbs) of chopped onion
1 small lemon
12 largish mushrooms (3 per person)
2oz (50g/4tbs) of fresh breadcrumbs
Chopped parsley
Salt and pepper
Nutmeg

Cream the butter with a wooden spoon, add the crushed garlic, finely chopped onion, lemon rind (finely grated) and juice, salt and pepper, nutmeg, parsley and breadcrumbs. Form the mixture into a roll and place in the fridge until it

hardens. Gently cook the mushrooms in a pan with a little butter for about a minute, just so they are partly cooked. Then place a thick slice of the garlic butter on top of each mushroom and put under a hot grill until brown on top. Serve immediately with lots of bread with which to soak up the tasty juices.

Cultivation: Garlic is cultivated, not a wild plant, and it was always said that it should be planted on the shortest day of the year and harvested on the longest. Divide the bulbs into separate cloves and plant these in a sunny bed.

Harvest: Dig it up when foliage withers, allow the outer skins to dry and then plait into a string.

HEARTSEASE

Botanical name: Viola tricolor
Alternative common name(s): Call-me-to-you, herb trinity, kiss-her-the-buttery, love in idleness, Pinkeney John, wild pansy
Part(s) used: Leaves and flowers
Description: This delightful wild annual is like a miniature pansy. Its name is derived from the belief that it is a remedy for a broken heart. Its many country names are testimony to its

Purple heartsease

popularity. Flowering from early spring to mid autumn, it has cream, yellow, blue, purple or tricoloured flowers and lanceolate, round-toothed leaves. Essentially a medicinal herb it is one that should always be used in its dried form. As an infusion, ointment or as a poultice it can be used to treat skin complaints such as acne, eczema or psoriasis – a poultice will reduce swelling and prevent bruising. As a mild laxative and a diuretic it is prescribed for urinary infections, as well as a cure for respiratory problems.

Cultivation: It seeds itself freely but seed can be sown indoors in trays or outdoors in the shade. Cuttings can be taken in summer. Like the sweet violet it prefers moist, rich, soil and sun or partial shade.

Harvest: Gather the leaves and flowers before they are fully out and dry quickly.

HORSETAIL

Botanical name: Equisetum arvense
Alternative common name(s): Bottlebrush, mare's tail, paddock pipes, pewterwort, shave grass
Part(s) used: Herb
Description: A relative of prehistoric plants of tree-like proportions, the horsetail grows to about 1ft(30cm) high in moist ground and is usually a sign of acid soil. Fossilized impressions of the plant have been found in coal which reveal that its shape has not changed since primeval times when it grew in vast forests. Extraordinarily hard to eradicate in the garden (only nasturtiums are said to smother and kill it off effectively) it grows from deeply bedded underground rhizomes that resemble dark brown string. It has two kinds of stem, the first in spring bears no vegetation just a cone-shaped head of spores, this is followed by a stem bearing pine needle-like leaves that grow in whorls up the stalk, similar to a bottlebrush. The first stem has the responsibility of propagating the plant, which it does most effectively in the manner of a fern or moss. It is the 'bottlebrush' stem which is of the greatest practical and medicinal use to man.

No other plant contains such a high degree of silica, a grit-like substance without which plants would droop. The needle-like leaves are dotted with mineral crystals and are imperceptible to the naked eye. The silica content has been put to good practical use over the centuries as an effective abrasive. Bunches of it were used to scour pots and polish brass and pewter.

The medicinal properties of the horsetail are numerous: it is a diuretic, healer of wounds and an astringent. It can be bought in pill form or can be made into a decoction. Two handfuls of the herb should be left to soak in 1pt (600ml/2½cups) of water for a few hours, before being brought to the boil and simmered for fifteen minutes, then left to infuse for a further ten minutes before being strained. The mixture should be kept in the fridge. The decoction, sniffed up the nose, will stop a nosebleed, or taken in small doses three times a day can be used to treat eczema and acne, as well as rheumatism and cystitis. Horsetail helps the body to absorb calcium and, taken internally or used externally, will rid the fingernails of white calcium marks in a few weeks and restore the shine to dull hair. A decoction can also be used as a good astringent skin lotion.

Cultivation: A wild perennial, it is best not encouraged in the garden but collected from the wild.

Harvest: Cut the bottlebrush stems during the growing season. The herb is more potent when fresh but it can be dried. If you choose to dry the herb take care not to damage the often brittle stems.

HOUSELEEK

Botanical name: Sempervivum tectorum
Alternative common name(s): Bullock's eye, Jupiter's eye or beard, sengren, Thor's beard
Part(s) used: Fresh leaves
Description: An ancient protection against lightning, fire and evil spells the houseleek would be planted on the roof of a house or grown in pots beside it. A native of the mountainous parts of southern and central Europe it was obviously introduced very early to this country for it bears

Equisetum arvense

Horsetail

an Anglo-Saxon name, *leac* or leek being the word for plant in the Dark Ages. The Roman's called it 'Jupiter's plant' due most probably to its strength and stubborn will to live in conditions that would make most plants blench and die. Like the Emperor Charlemagne who decreed that all in his empire should grow it as a protective device on their roofs, the Romans also believed in its magical powers. In certain rural areas of Europe today, where ancient superstitions have survived, there is still a reluctance to remove it from the roof of a dwelling.

The tight rosettes of succulent leaves, sharp pointed and edged with hairs, make an eye-catching pattern of swirling shapes, one rosette almost nudging another out of place, not a centimetre of space being left between them. They are so perfectly formed that they almost appear man-made, only the 4-5in (10-13cm) stem topped by a head of pink flowers in July, giving them a more 'natural' look.

The houseleek is the most accommodating of plants, needing little water and even less soil, an ideal candidate for the top of a wall or a rockery. They grow particularly well on a thatched roof, look charming lapping over the edges of a terracotta pot or spilling over the sides of an ornamental stone bowl. Used in such a way they can make a stylish feature at the centre of a formal herb or flower garden, and one that does not require constant attention.

As much valued for its medicinal as its magical properties the herb has been used as a remedy for centuries. The leaves are amazingly succulent, considering where they grow and can be pulped or bruised and applied as an antiseptic to a burn, cut or inflamed part of the body. They can also be used to soothe the pain of a nettle rash, bee sting and insect bite. Simply pick one of the larger outer leaves, squeeze it between forefinger and thumb and apply to the affected part. Culpeper wrote that 'The juice takes away warts and corns in the hands or feet, being often bathed therewith and the skin of the leaves laid on them afterwards' and that the 'leaves bruised and laid upon the crown of the head, stays bleeding at the nose quickly'. Mixed with honey the bitter juice is a remedy for thrush in the mouth, but avoid using it in large quantities as it is a powerful emetic. The juice can also be squeezed from the leaf into the eyes, its antiseptic properties acting as a preventative against styes at the same time as cooling any inflammation.

Cultivation: Increase by detaching the offsets. They will grow where they are placed, whether on the roof or a wall with shallow, damp soil. It may take a while for the plant to 'take' and multiply.

Harvest: Being evergreen, hence the name *Sempervivum* (*tectorum* meaning 'roof'), they can be harvested fresh throughout the year.

HYSSOP

Botanical name: Hyssopus officinalis
Part(s) used: Flowers and young leaves
Description: This evergreen member of the mint family was once regarded as a symbol of purification and was used in the ritual cleansings of churches and leprous houses. A native of southern Europe where it grew on dry, stony ground, it was most probably introduced to the British Isles by the Romans and went on to become an important ingredient of monastery infirmary gardens.

Now a delightful, old-fashioned addition, to a herb garden it is grown for its medicinal, aromatic and aesthetic qualities rather than for culinary use. Its flavour is exceptionally strong and though it effectively disguised the rancid taste of far from fresh meat in times past, it is now considered too overpowering to be appreciated in the kitchen, though it is employed in the making of liqueurs such as Benedictine and Chartreuse and is said to bring out the flavour of apricots. The strong scent of the plant justified its use as a strewing herb and it became an important addition to fragrant nosegays – the volatile oil it produces is still a favourite with perfumers. Because it retains its scent when dried it can also be used in pot-pourri and herb pillows.

A shrubby perennial growing to about 2ft (60cm) high, it has long thin, sharp-pointed leaves and, depending on the variety, blue, purple, pink or white flowers. These are borne

Hyssop

from June to October, the long flowering season recommends it being grown in both herb and ornamental gardens. Old-fashioned, low-growing, mazes and knot gardens were frequently composed of hyssop and its low, hedge-like habit, makes it suitable for edging paths or formal beds – in the manner of dwarf box. Hyssop has woody stems, and it does not always take kindly to being cut hard back, so it might require replanting every four or five years. It acts as a magnet to bees as well as butterflies.

As a medicinal plant hyssop has expectorant, stimulant, carminative and antiseptic qualities. It is best taken as a tea made of the fresh or dried flowering tips: cover 1oz (28g/2tbs) of the fresh herb or 1½-2tsp of the dried herb with 2pt (1⅕l/5cups) of boiling water. Drunk several times a day this mixture will relieve the symptoms of flu and colds by provoking a sweat and so lowering the temperature; it also makes an excellent gargle for a sore throat. Gerard reckoned that 'Hyssope made with figges, water, honey and rue and drunken, helpeth the old cough' and for centuries the herb has been used as a remedy for catarrh and respiratory tract troubles in general. As an antiseptic it will cleanse the system and can be used to treat anaemia. Made into a poultice it is a remedy for bruising; Parkinson wrote that it was used to heal cuts, bruising, and fresh wounds 'eyther alone or with sugar.' When added to a bath it will relieve rheumatic pain. It should not be used by epileptics in quantity or on a regular basis by anyone as the herb contains a chemical called ketones which has a toxic effect on the nervous system.

Cultivation: Grow from seed sown in spring or from cuttings taken during the summer. It will tolerate semi shade but prefers a sunny position and well-drained soil.

Harvest: Gather the flowering tips and use fresh or dry.

LADY'S MANTLE

Botanical name: Alchemilla vulgaris
Alternative common name(s): Lions' foot, bear's foot, nine hooks

Part(s) used: Herb and root
Description: A hardy perennial that grows in northern temperate climes, lady's mantle grows no higher than 12in (30cm). It has rounded, lobed and downy leaves that seem to have been cut around with a miniature pair of pinking shears. From early summer until autumn it produces panicles of tiny lime-green flowers without petals.

Early in the morning, what appear to be drops of dew collect in the furrows of the leaves. Horses and sheep are said to find the plant tasty but they will not touch it until these 'dew drops' have disappeared. Resembling minute crystal balls the sparkling drops of moisture are produced by the plant itself and were thought to have magical powers in the Middle Ages. Known as 'water from Heaven' the drops would be carefully collected and used by an alchemist in his search for the philosopher's stone. Hence this dainty little plant bears the Latin name *Alchemilla*, which is derived from the word alchemy. The common name, lady's mantle, has its origins in the Middle Ages when it was one of the many plants dedicated to the Virgin Mary.

An astringent and styptic, it was used to help contract and dry wounds. Culpeper discovered that lady's mantle was a good remedy for women's complaints:

It is one of the most singular wound herbs and therefore highly prized and praised by the Germans who use it in all wounds inward and outward, to drink the decoction thereof and wash the wounds therewith, or dip tents therein and put them into the wounds which wonderfully drieth up all humidity of the sores and abateth inflammations therein. It quickly healeth all green wounds, not suffering any corruption to remain behind and curest old sores, though fistulous and hollow.

Today it is used in the form of an infusion which can stimulate the appetite and also act as an effective treatment for excessive menstruation and diarrhoea. A decoction of the fresh or dried root will also staunch bleeding of any sort.

Being astringent, an infusion of the dried

Lady's mantle

leaves, or the juice from the fresh, is an excellent treatment for open pores or acne. Extract the juice from the fresh leaves and stalks either in a juice extractor or blender, then strain the liquid off through muslin or a coffee filter. Apply to the face and allow to dry, then rinse off with tepid water. A variety of lady's mantle, *Alchemilla mollis*, is a charming garden plant and, happily, one that seeds itself freely. It makes an excellent edging subject and when it seeds itself in paths it is more often than not left as an attractive addition. Its pale, limey green, frothy, head of flowers lights up any dark corner and offsets to perfection brightly coloured flowering plants. A favourite with flower arrangers, both fresh or dried, it is the sort of plant that can make blooms go a long way.

Cultivation: Sow seed in flowering position or divide roots in spring or autumn. Tolerating moist soil, it prefers to be planted in light shade.

Harvest: Either use fresh or harvest the leaves, root and flowers in June and July for drying.

LAVENDER

Botanical name: Lavandula species
Part(s) used: Flowers and leaves
Description: It is difficult to imagine an English garden without lavender and though it is a native of the western region of the Mediterranean it is, surprisingly, the English lavender, *Lavandula vera*, that has the strongest fragrance of all. Although an attractive plant in itself, especially the dark purple 'Dwarf Munstead' and 'Hidcote' varieties, it is for its deliciously warm and sweet aroma that it is grown, both in the garden and commercially for the essential oil. The oil is extracted from the flowers as well as the stalks.

Lavender has been grown in this country for centuries and though there is no record of the Romans having introduced it, it is likely that they did so. It was certainly popular in pre-Dissolution monasteries. Gerard and Parkinson write of it in relation to their own gardens and it was listed as one of the herbs taken to the New World by the Pilgrim Fathers.

The fragrance has always been enjoyed and used not only to scent linen, clothes and the body – the Latin word *Lavandus* meaning 'to be washed' – but sweeten the atmosphere. It also had its culinary uses for a lavender conserve was a particular favourite of Queen Elizabeth 1 and, in a powdered form, took its place on the table alongside salt and pepper to be sprinkled on savoury dishes. Tastes and habits change but lavender is still an important culinary herb and can make an original addition to a salad, the fresh young leaves and tiny individual flowers adding colour as well as flavour. **Note:** the French lavender, *Lavandula stoechas*, is highly toxic and should never be eaten.

A little over a hundred years ago English lavender was grown on a vast scale in Mitcham in Surrey, a successful field would yield up to 20lb (9kg) of oil, but these fields are now covered with suburban housing, the only English lavender fields are now found in Norfolk.

Renowned as an anti-depressant, it is an excellent remedy for anxiety and nervous headaches. Used as a massage oil it will relax the muscles wonderfully as well as uplift the depressed spirits. The oil or water can be used directly on the skin or an infusion of 1oz (28g/2tbs) of fresh or dried flowers to 1pt (600ml/2½cups) of water may be taken internally.

A bath spiced with a strong infusion of lavender combats fatigue as does lavender water smoothed on the temples.

Lavender water
3 large tablespoons of lavender flowers
4 fl oz (110ml/½cup) of white wine vinegar
2 fl oz (56ml/¼cup) of rose water

Place all the ingredients in a container and seal. Leave in the dark for several weeks and shake regularly. Strain before using.

Lavender is popular with bees and there are several different varieties from which to choose, though it is the English lavender, *Lavandula vera*, that was grown commercially for its oil and is most suitable for the herb garden. It has green rather than silver foliage whereas the *Lavandula spica* or Old English lavender has silver and grows to quite a size. There are dwarf compact kinds of

Lavender

Lavandula spica such as 'Hidcote' which has voilet blue flowers and 'Munstead' which has deep violet blue flowers. *Lavandula stoechas* or French lavender is unusual in that it has purple bracts emerging from the top of the spikes of flowers.

Cultivation: An evergreen shrubby perennial, it can be grown from seed, certain varieties self seeding with ease. Germination can be disappointing but if the seed is put in the fridge for several weeks before sowing partial success will follow. It can also be propagated by heel cuttings taken in August or softwood cuttings in spring. It should be cut back lightly after flowering to prevent it from becoming leggy, but should not be cut hard until the spring – pruning at this time of the year encourages bushy new growth from the base.

Harvest: Cut the stem of the flowers for drying before they open, usually in July, and lay flat or hang up to dry.

LOVAGE

Botanical name: Levisticum officinale
Alternative common name(s): Love parsley
Part(s) used: Leaves, seeds, young stems and root
Description: A long-lived perennial that can grow up to 4ft (1.2m) tall, the leaves of lovage are similar to those of celery, but stronger, a darker green and shiny. Large umbels of tiny yellow flowers are borne on hollow stems, the following seeds being brown. Every part of the plant has an aroma that can be likened to yeast but the flavour is strongly reminiscent of celery, is warmer and has a dash of curry and parsley thrown in. The unique flavour of this marvellous culinary herb makes it a favourite of all keen cooks, as those unfamiliar with it always enjoy its intriguing aroma. One plant is quite sufficient as lovage grows to a considerable size and apart from its practical uses, can make an attractive and bold statement in the back of a border.

A native of mountainous Mediterranean regions, it was a favourite culinary and bath herb of the Greeks and Romans, the latter being responsible for its spread throughout their empire. It once had a reputation as an aphrodisiac or love charm, hence the name, but

is no longer considered as such today. It does have medicinal properties: an infusion made of the leaves, seeds or root is a remedy for a fever, upset stomach, jaundice, urinary problems or delayed menstruation. Used as a gargle it will soothe a sore throat. A mild antiseptic and digestive, it is also a diuretic and consequently should not be taken by pregnant women.

It was listed as one of the essential medicinal herbs grown in the ninth century Swiss Benedictine monastery of St Gall and it was also popular as a bath and culinary herb of the Tudors and Stuarts. Then, as now, the leaves and seeds as well as the young root, whose flavour can be likened to celeriac, were used to flavour salads, soups and stews.

The following soup can be eaten hot or cold, has a subtle and intriguing flavour to the uninitiated and makes excellent use of an over-bountiful crop of courgettes.

Lovage and courgette soup
2 large potatoes
4 – 6 medium-sized courgettes
1 large onion
1 tbs of oil
2½pt (1.5l/6cups) of chicken stock
1 clove of garlic crushed
1 tbs of chopped lovage leaves
Salt and pepper

Cook the onion in the oil and garlic and add the peeled and chopped potatoes and sliced courgettes. When partially cooked pour in the stock and chopped lovage leaves and simmer until all the ingredients are soft. Place in a blender and then flavour with salt and pepper to taste. Serve hot or cold, garnished with chopped lovage leaves or a dash of cream.

Cultivation: Sow the ripe seed in the autumn or divide the roots in spring. It is an easy plant to grow and though it prefers a moist soil will tolerate most situations. It will live for several years if cut well back in the autumn and given a generous feed.

Harvest: Pick the leaves before the plant comes into flower when they are young and not too tough, and dry or freeze. Gather the seed when it is fresh. The young stems can be candied like angelica.

MARIGOLD

Botanical name: Calendula officinalis
Alternative common name(s): Golds, pot marigold
Part(s) used: Flowers
Description: This brilliant hardy annual with its orange daisy-like flowers and pale green, long and hairy leaves is now thought of as a classic cottage garden plant but it is, in fact, a native of southern Europe and of India. The pot marigold is the true herb and has the medicinal properties.

Its long flowering period from early summer until cut down by frosts in late autumn have influenced its name, the Latin word *calendulae* meaning 'throughout the months'. Marigolds were also once called Mary buds and were assigned to the Virgin Mary, though in the Middle Ages they symbolized jealousy which is not such a happy association. So popular were they as a pot herb that Gerard noted in his herbal that the dried petals were stored for sale in barrels. These were used to decorate, flavour and colour food and could be called the poor man's saffron. They were used in soups and stews, to which they added a hot spicy taste, and they did, and still do, make a colourful addition to a salad both green or rice.

In America the religious sect the Shakers who grew and sold herbs and herbal remedies on a vast scale in the nineteenth century, believed they were an effective cure for gangrene and there is no doubt that they have antiseptic as well as antibacterial qualities. The dried petals are an effective healing agent with which to treat burns and cysts and have a good reputation for soothing internal and external ulcers either in the form of a poultice or an infusion. The flowers are remedies for eczema and acne and can also be used to treat heart disorders, induce a delayed period and soothe menstrual pain but should not be taken during pregnancy.

An infusion of the petals, marigold tea, can be taken after an accident to bring out bruises and so prevent internal wounds from causing problems – the flowers have a beneficial effect on the arteries

and veins. Culpeper, assigning the herb to the sun, comments that 'marigolds are very expulsive and little less effective in small-pox and measles than saffron'.

Marigold has always been valued as a cosmetic herb and an infusion makes a good astringent and disinfectant lotion for an oily skin, helping to close open pores – it was also once used as a hair dye. It has a soothing effect on scalp conditions, though William Turner, often called the 'Father of English Botany', wryly says in his sixteenth-century herbal that 'Summe use to make theyr here yellow with the floure of the herbe, not being content with the naturall colour which God hath given them'.

The following oil will soften rough skin and can also be used to soothe sunburn and eczema.

Marigold oil
1½oz (1cup) of marigold petals
12 fl oz (1½cups) of almond oil

Put the petals in a sealed container with the almond oil and place in a warm, light position. Leave for several weeks, adding more petals as they sink to the bottom of the container. Strain through muslin and bottle.

Cultivation: Sow the seeds in the late spring, preferably in a sunny position as they are apt to become leggy in the shade. They will tolerate any soil and self seed freely.

Harvest: Pick the flowers when they are open, and use fresh or dry.

MARJORAM

Botanical name:
Wild or common marjoram *Origanum vulgare*
Sweet or knotted marjoram *Origanum majorana*
Pot marjoram *Origanum onites*
Part(s) used: Herb and leaves
Description: A member of the mint family, there are many different varieties of marjoram and oregano, the one frequently being mistaken for the other. Wild and pot marjoram are both hardy perennials, while sweet marjoram is a half-hardy annual. All three can be used as culinary herbs, the wild and pot marjoram have a sharp warm flavour; the sweet marjoram has preservative

Lovage

qualities. Wild marjoram is the one most often used as a medicinal herb though pot marjoram also has healing properties. Marjoram is one of the most ancient and widely used of all herbs; it grows to about 2ft (60cm) high and has tight 'knotted' heads of insignificant pink or creamy flowers from August to October and small ovate leaves that are rich in volatile oil.

The botanical name *Origanum* means 'Joy of the Mountain' and its scent certainly justifies such a delightful name. The ancient Greeks used it in their winding-sheets and believed that if it grew beside a grave it was a sign that the deceased was happy. They also garlanded their brides and bridegrooms with the herb to ensure that 'they lived happily ever after'. Our ancestors used it as a strewing herb and in knots, the golden marjoram *O. vulgare* 'Aureum' being an attractive and popular plant in the ornamental garden today, adding a bright splash of yellowy green in between paving stones or at the front of a border.

As a medicinal herb it is a remedy for a host of problems. It is a tonic, digestive and a diuretic, will stimulate the appetite the calm the nerves. Because it provokes perspiration it is a good remedy for flu, bronchitis and the common cold, an infusion being equally effective as a sedative with which to combat seasickness.

In the kitchen it is invaluable and has been used in Britain to flavour food well before any records were kept. It is excellent in soups and stuffings, and is a classic ingredient of bouquet garni and Italian pasta and many other dishes. For a quick and tasty supper dish or for something different to take on a picnic, try the following:

French bread pizzas
1 large French loaf
1 Mozzarella cheese
1 tin of anchovy fillets
4 large peeled tomatoes
1tbs of fresh marjoram, chopped
Olive oil
Salt and pepper

Cut the loaf in half along the length, sprinkle with olive oil, then cover with a layer of tomatoes, Mozzarella, anchovy fillets, marjoram and season with salt and pepper. Bake in a moderate oven until the cheese has melted. Cut into 8 pieces.

An infusion of the fresh herb used as a rinse will condition the hair and a fragrant and refreshing bath oil can be made by adding, to a base of almond oil, a few drops of the volatile oil of marjoram and lavender. It is a delightfully aromatic addition to pot-pourri and for those who enjoy drying their own flowers for arrangements its dark colouring is very useful even though the flowers are not showy in themselves.

Cultivation: Marjoram prefers a dry, light soil and a sunny position. Sow seed under glass in early spring or grow from stem cuttings taken before the plant flowers. Roots can also be divided. Sweet marjoram is tender so should, if possible, be overwintered under glass.

Harvest: Gather the leaves in summer before the plant comes into flower.

MARSHMALLOW

Botanical name: Althaea officinalis
Alternative common name(s): Mallards, marsh mallice, mauls, schloss tea
Part(s) used: Leaves, flowers, roots
Description: Growing, as the name suggests, in salt marshes and damp fertile places, the marshmallow is one of the most attractive of wild plants and one that also looks striking planted to the back of the border in the cultivated garden. A hardy perennial that grows 3-4ft (over 1m) tall, it has fleshy, downy leaves and pretty pale pink, five-petalled, flowers that appear from August to September. The roots are long and parsnip like, have a sugary flavour and are the most mucilaginous parts of the herb that is famed for its emollient qualities.

A native of many European countries and parts of Africa and Asia, it was believed by some to flourish only at the gates of happy homes and has enjoyed a long and good reputation as a soothing and healing plant for centuries. Its mucilage content, 35% in the root and 10% in the leaves, causes it to produce a gelatinous-like substance that, though no longer used to make those deliciously squidgy pink and white edible cushions, inspired their name.

Marshmallow

A decoction of the dried root or infusion of the leaves, 1oz (28g/2tbs) to 1pt (600ml/2½cups) of water, can be taken as a remedy for a stubborn dry cough, sore throat and bronchitis, will calm an upset stomach, combat constipation and soothe cystitus. The mucilage coats the stomach and urinary tract and so calms the condition. Nicholas Culpeper extols its virtues extensively and like many of his fellow herbalists recommends it to ease the passage of kidney and other stones, as a cure for constipation and to reduce swelling and inflammation. He considered it an excellent preventative for hair loss and adds that 'If the feet be washed in the decoction, it will draw the rheum from the head'.

The Romans ate the root as a vegetable. Curiously those about to undergo torture by hot irons would paint their skin with an ointment of mallow sap, white of egg and plantain seeds, though how they obtained the ingredients while under guard is a mystery. A coating of this ointment would lessen the effects of the burns and so hopefully prove their innocence. Teething babies were also given a stick or root of mallow to suck to 'cool' their inflamed gums, it is conveniently sweet as well as soothing. The freshly crushed leaf can be rubbed on an insect bite or bee sting to lessen the pain and inflammation and a warm poultice of the dried leaves or crushed fresh root will serve to draw boils to a head.

Cultivation: Sow seed in trays in late spring or early summer or divide roots in the autumn or winter. It likes a moist, rich soil and full sun.

Harvest: Gather the leaves before the plant flowers, the flowers in August and the root when it is at its most potent during the late autumn and winter and then dry.

MEADOWSWEET

Botanical name: Filipendula ulmaria
Alternative common name(s): Bridewort, dolloff, lady-of-the-meadow, maidsweet, queen-of-the-meadows
Part(s) used: Herb
Description: In 1640 John Parkinson wrote in his book *The Theatre of Plants* that 'Queen Elizabeth

of famous memory did more desire it than any other sweet herbe to strew her chambers withall' and one can understand why. The large fuzzy head of creamy white flowers certainly have a deliciously strong scent that is similar to almonds, while the leaves have a fresher, almost cucumber-like fragrance. It was originally a sacred herb of the Druids and an old custom was to strew meadowsweet on the floor of the church and dwelling where a wedding was to be celebrated, and to twine it into a garland for the bride, hence its common name bridewort.

Frequently seen growing beside streams, in hedgerows and in damp meadows where the

Meadowsweet

Meadowsweet

ground is not acid, it reaches up to 4ft (1.2m) high and is a perennial with reddish purple stems. Its dark green leaves have downy undersides and somewhat wrinkled leaves hence the specific name *ulmaria* which means elm like, while the name *Filipendula* comes from the word *filum* or thread which describes the hair-like roots attached to the rhizomatous rootstock.

The top heavy head of flowers is made up of tiny florets that do not bear nectar and so rely on insects that are attracted by their scent for fertilization. These were once dried to make a tea which, flavoured with honey, was used to clear a stuffy head. The taste of both the leaves and flowers is not unpleasant and was used to flavour wines and beers and, being rich in vitamin C, makes a healthy addition to a salad. According to Culpeper and Gerard, both the scent and taste of meadowsweet 'makes the heart merry and joyful and delighteth the senses'.

In 1838 salicylic acid was discovered and meadowsweet was found to be a rich source. Consequently it played its part in the discovery of the drug aspirin that was first formulated by Charles Frederic Gerhardt in 1853, and found to be such an excellent antidote to pain. The effect of the natural herbal remedies derived from meadowsweet is similar to the chemical drug and can be taken to bring down a fever, disperse the uric acid which forms crystals in the joints and so soothe the inflammation. It can be taken as a remedy for colds and influenza, high blood pressure and other blood disorders. The simplest method of using the herb is as an infusion:

Pour 1pt (600ml/2½cups) of hot, not boiling, water on to a dessertspoonful (7ml/2tsp) of the dried or fresh leaves or flowers. Allow to infuse for ten minutes and then strain. This infusion is an excellent remedy for those suffering from diarrhorea, especially children, and can be taken in wine-glass doses three times a day.

Cultivation: As happy in the shade as it is in the sun, it prefers a moist rich soil. Seed can be sown in autumn or spring where it is to flower or the roots divided in the spring.

Harvest: Gather the flowers and leaves when the plant is flowering in July and dry them separately.

MINT

Botanical name: Mentha
Part(s) used: Herb
Description: Only parsley can rival the popularity of mint in the garden and kitchen – it is frequently the first herb to be planted in a new garden. It also boasts almost as many different varieties as thyme. Walafred Strabo writing in the ninth century noted 'Mints I grow in abundance and in all its varieties. How many they are. I might as well try to count the sparks from Vulcan's furnace beneath Etna!' Though not a native plant it was most probably introduced to this country by the Romans who valued it highly as a strewing and bath herb. Garlands of mint were thought to stimulate inspiration and concentration, though the Greeks forbade their soldiers to eat it, believing that it stimulated their libido and romantic inclinations.

The different varieties of mint vary in flavour but, in general, they all have the same medicinal uses. They are antibacterial and sweat inducing and consequently used to treat coughs, colds and influenza and were thought to protect those that carried it from being infected by lepers and those suffering from the plague. Culpeper deemed mint 'Very profitable to the stomach' there being few remedies of greater efficacy for vomiting, wind, bad breath, child bearing, sore gums and toothache. A wonderfully varied list! As a cooling herb, when the oil, being menthol, is applied to the skin it acts as a mild anaesthetic and so is frequently used as a massage for rheumatism and sprains. Menthol oil is re-nowned, of course, for its ability to clear the respiratory tract but should be used with discretion.

Mint is adept at stimulating the appetite, its culinary uses having as beneficial effect on the health as its flavour on the taste buds. Mint is the traditional accompaniment to roast lamb, the herb serving to offset the sometimes indigestible quality of the young meat. One of the best loved and versatile of all culinary herbs, it is widely used in drinks, sweets, sauces, relishes, as well as a garnish. New potatoes would be an impoverished vegetable without it; chopped into ice

Mint

cubes it is a wonderfully refreshing addition to summer drinks and mixed with yoghurt it is a cooling accompaniment to hot and spicy eastern dishes.

Mint sorbet makes a light and delicate finale to a rich meal and is a great standby in the freezer.

Mint sorbet
8 large sprigs of tender mint
½pt (280ml/1¼cups) of water
Juice of 1 lemon
1 egg white
4oz (125g/1¼cups) of castor sugar

Dissolve the sugar in the water and having added the mint (being careful to check that no woody bits have been included) leave to cool. Then add the lemon juice and place in the freezer. When nearly frozen stir in beaten egg white and return to the freezer. Serve with a sprig of fresh mint.

Another very simple to make and always popular recipe is for home-made lemonade:

Blend a handful of fresh mint leaves and one heaped tablespoon of sugar and three sliced lemons with 2pt (1l/5cups) of water. Leave standing for an hour and then strain. Add ice and garnish glasses with lemon peel and a sprig of mint.

Mice hate the smell of mint so it is a good herb to plant around a potting shed where vegetables are stored. It is a good companion plant and effectively repels cabbage grubs and flies.

The following varieties of mint are useful and/ or attractive additions to the herb and vegetable garden:

PEPPERMINT, *Mentha piperita,* commonly called brandy mint is one of the most common varieties. It grows up to 2ft (60cm) high with whorls of pale lilac flowers and smooth, toothed, leaves.

SPEARMINT, *Mentha spicata,* commonly called garden mint is the most popular culinary mint, it has a warm, sweet flavour. Used in toothpaste and chewing gum it has wrinkled bright green leaves and pale pinkish lilac flowers.

BLACK PEPPERMINT, *Mentha piperita vulgaris,* is good for drying and makes a fine tea.

APPLE MINT, *Mentha suaveolens,* commonly known as Egyptian mint smells of mint and apples. It was always grown in monastery gardens and was once known as monks' herb. It is the variety used in traditional mint sauce.

PINEAPPLE MINT, *Mentha rotundifolia variegata,* has a creamy variegated foliage and a pleasant apple scent.

GINGER MINT, *Mentha x gentilis* 'Variegata', has an attractive yellow variegation which gave it its name, as it smells of apple not ginger.

BOWLES MINT, *Mentha rotundifolia* 'Bowles' is a relation of the apple mint and a good culinary herb.

EAU DE COLOGNE MINT, *Mentha citrata,* commonly called bergamot mint is used in the making of cosmetics and fragrant products such as pot-pourri. The leaves are tinged with purple and the herb is only used sparingly in medicine and in the kitchen.

WATER MINT, *Mentha aquatica,* has a stronger flavour that is not quite as pleasant as the others. It grows wild beside rivers and ditches.

PENNYROYAL, *Mentha pulegium,* is a prostrate, pungent, plant with small leaves. Ancients used it as a fumigatory herb and it was the most widely used medicinal mint, though it should not be taken internally if you are pregnant or have a kidney complaint.

Cultivation: Mint is best not grown from seed as it does not breed true or can be sterile. Plants should be propagated by dividing the root runners. One of the most invasive of herbs, it should be grown in a pot or window-box or set in a bottomless pot set into the ground. It prefers a moist soil and when grown in the shade, produces foliage with a stronger flavour and scent. It is vulnerable to rust which is incurable. When the orange spots are detected on the leaves, they should be cut and straw placed over the plant and burnt. Plant well away from other herbs and place in a different position every four years to obtain good results. Mint varieties are greedy and should have a regular dressing of fertilizer.

Harvest: Cut the leaves and flowers in summer when the flowers are in bud and dry or freeze. The leaves can also be preserved in honey, oil or vinegar.

NASTURTIUM

Botanical name: Trapaeolum majus
Alternative common name(s): Indian cress
Part(s) used: Leaves, flowers and seeds
Description: The nasturtium is said to have arisen from the spilt blood of a Trojan warrior, the round leaves being his shield and the trumpet-shaped flower his helmet. In reality it originated in South America and was brought to Europe by the Spanish *conquistadores*. Gerard in 1597 writes of it having been sent to him by the botanist John Robin of France and its popularity was immediate, due, most probably, to it being so accommodating a plant. Parkinson recommended its use along with carnations and gilliflowers in the making of fragrant tussie mussies or posies and John Evelyn extolled the virtues of its seed as a treatment for scurvy.

A perennial in its native habitat it is treated as an annual here, is ridiculously easy to grow, undemanding and rewarding. A trailing and sometimes climbing plant, it has round flat leaves and long spurred flowers of brilliant orange that are followed by large green seeds. There is now an extensive list of varieties from which to choose. There are those with double blooms or variegated foliage, the leaves veined prettily with cream, as well as a wide colour range of flowers. Seed of dwarf, compact, trailing and climbing varieties can be bought with flowers of pale cream spotted with scarlet, through lemons and oranges to cherry red and deep mahogany. Because they flower better on poor rather than fertile soil, they are indispensable to the gardener who has problem areas. They will successfully cover an unsightly hump or bump, smother an area of rough ground or can be used to trail from a window-box or tub. Any child wishing to start a garden or grow a flower from seed should be encouraged to cut their teeth on the nasturtium. The seed is easy to handle, it seldom fails to germinate and grows fast to a rewardingly large

size. The fact that it can be eaten as well as picked for decoration recommends it even further.

Rich in vitamin C, it can be eaten to promote a healthy, clear, skin and shining eyes, though nasturtium is a strong herb and should not be consumed in great quantities. Place a few leaves in a sandwich or chop a few of the flowers and leaves into a salad. The flavour is peppery and the seed heads when dry can be used in the same way as peppercorns and ground to season food. For centuries they have been a substitute for capers; pick them young and simmer them very gently in spiced vinegar in a covered pan for an hour, leave to cool and then bottle.

The plant has an unusually high sulphur content and the flowers and leaves when made into a lotion will prevent hair loss, promote growth and condition the scalp. Chop up a large handful of flowers and leaves and put in a wide-necked bottle filled with ⅓pt (225ml/1cup) of alcohol and replace the stopper. Place in a warm dark place and shake daily for two weeks, then strain and add a few drops of a fragrant essential oil such as lavender. Rub or brush into the scalp regularly.

A natural antibiotic, the herb, unlike a chemical drug, has the added advantage of not destroying the intestinal flora and an infusion of the fresh leaves can be taken as a remedy for bronchial and catarrhal conditions.

Cultivation: Sow the seed where it is to flower in the spring, in well-drained soil. It is a good companion plant and will protect others from pests though it is itself prone to attack by blackfly.

Harvest: Pick the flowers and leaves during the summer, the leaves before the flowers appear if they are to be dried. The seeds should be collected when they have swelled.

NETTLE, STINGING

Botanical name: Urtica dioica
Alternative common name(s): Devil's leaf, devil's plaything, stinging nettle, tanging nettle

Stinging nettle with dandelion and morning glory

Part(s) used: Leaves
Description: This must be one herb that needs no description for it grows everywhere and is far from fussy as to position or conditions; though it seems particularly attracted to cultivated land and the ground around dwellings. One indisputable fact is that it enriches the soil in which it grows and consequently is a valuable companion plant, particularly to certain soft fruits such as raspberries (see 'Companion Plants').

The whole plant is covered with hairs that contain formic acid, the nettles 'stinging' agent. Happily, it supplies its own cure as the juice rubbed on an affected part of the body, will, like dock leaves, relieve the pain. So many benefits can be derived from this unjustly abhorred weed that it is hard to understand (its sting excepted) how it came to acquire such a bad reputation.

As a native of all temperate regions it has been put to good use for centuries, the Romans would beat their legs with the herb as a means to ward off the chill and improve their circulation. The roots and stems were woven into cloth and made into paper and used to make a pleasingly bright green and yellow dye. The generic name *Urtica* comes from the Latin word to burn, *uro*, which gave a warning to those not used to handling the plant; but if clasped with gloves and cut with a pair of scissors or a knife, it can be put to many excellent uses, both medicinal and culinary.

The seed given in mash to poultry was an old country method of improving their condition and encouraging them to lay. It was also fed to horses to revive their spirit and add gloss to their coats. Beating the body with nettles was a popular remedy for rheumatism and taken internally it has a good reputation as a blood purifier. Stimulating, astringent and toning it relieves anaemia and arthritis, is said to help those wishing to slim and 'Strengthen the will and earth dreamy subjects'. An infusion can be made of the leaves or seeds and taken regularly in wineglass doses but the most palatable way of using the herb is as a tasty vegetable, similar in many respects to spinach. Treat as spinach and include a few sorrel or dandelion leaves to add extra flavour. Pick the leaves when young and tender as when old they are apt to be bitter. Rinse them under cold water and plunge into a pan of salted boiling water until tender, strain and add a knob of butter. The water in which the nettles were boiled can be saved and taken as a tonic, or make a soup which ensures that none of the herbs beneficial properties are lost. Rich in vitamin C it also contains mucilage and valuable minerals such as iron. Wash the nettles and braise in butter seasoned with crushed garlic, adding some diced potato and chicken stock. Blend, season and serve hot or cold.

The juice, being a coagulant, can be used to seal gaps and cracks in wooden tubs and the 'tea' or water in which fresh nettles have been soaked for several weeks, makes an excellent and cheap, organic liquid fertilizer. Packed along with fruit such as plums it will also preserve their bloom. But as any naturalist will appreciate, one of the major arguments for giving the nettle garden space, is the fact that it is an invaluable source of food for the small tortoiseshell, peacock and red admiral caterpillars.

Cultivation: Collect seed from the wild and sow in the spring or divide roots at any time of the year.

Harvest: Gather the seeds when they are ripe and dry and the herb in May or June before it flowers, then dry or freeze. If frozen, do not thaw before using but cook directly or infuse in boiling water.

PARSLEY

Botanical name: Petroselinum crispum
Alternative common name(s): Persely, persele, petersylinge
Part(s) used: Herb
Description: The best known and most commonly used of herbs in this country, this superbly versatile hardy biennial was introduced to this country from southern Europe in the sixteenth century. The flat-leafed variety was the first known here and though this Italian or French parsley, *Petroselinum neapolitanum*, has a stronger flavour, it is the curled-leafed variety that is most widely grown. Hamburg parsley, *Petroselinum tuberosum*, has never attained the popularity of the others, even though its parsnip-like tap root

73

Apium Petroselinum

Published by D.ᵣ Woodville March.1. 1791.

Parsley

has the flavour of celeriac. It can be eaten as a vegetable or grated to add flavour to various dishes, but the coarse foliage, though edible, has little to recommend it.

Originally revered by the ancient Greeks as a sacred rather than a culinary herb, parsley was an important adjunct to funeral ceremonies. It was thought to have sprung up from the spilt blood of the forerunner of death, Archemorus. A more glamorous use of the herb was as a wreath with which the victors of the Isthmian Games were adorned.

Many superstitions surround the sowing and growing of the herb, these change from region to region. It is not difficult to understand how these old wives' tales came into being for parsley is notoriously awkward to germinate, the process taking up to eight weeks. It also hates to be transplanted – it will react by coming into flower which causes the foliage to deteriorate.

Many thought, and continue to believe, that it is unlucky to offer a plant as a gift or to move it to a new house, others think that only children should sow the seed, that curses should be muttered while doing so and that it will only consent to germinate if the woman of the house 'wears the pants'. There is also a legend that it has to go to the devil seven times and return before it begins to grow and that it will only do so if sown by an honest man.

Used as a medicinal herb it can help stimulate the digestive system and reduce flatulence. Being a mild diuretic it will treat those suffering from kidney stones and will benefit the circulation. An infusion of the fresh leaves applied to the skin regularly is thought to improve, at the same time as rid, the complexion of freckles and moles.

Rich in vitamins A, B and C, it is an important ingredient of any diet, raw or cooked. Its volatile oil is extremely strong and consequently the herb should always be added towards the end of any cooking process or simply used as a garnish. It is famed for its power to mask the smell of garlic on the breath. Parsley vinaigrette is a delicious accompaniment to cold ham. Simply blend together the following ingredients:

8oz (250g/2½cups) of fresh parsley leaves
2 peeled garlic cloves
1tsp of French mustard
2tsp of castor sugar
2tbs (28ml) of white wine vinegar
1tbs (15ml) of lemon juice
½pt (280ml/1¼cups) of olive oil

Cultivation: Soak the seed (it should be no older than 1 year) for 24 hours before sowing it *in situ* in spring, summer or autumn. Immediately after sowing, water with a kettle of boiling water. The roots prefer to be kept cool so partial shade is tolerated and a rich soil preferred.

Harvest: Cut the leaves before the plant flowers and if the flavour is to be preserved, freeze rather than dry. Harvest the seeds in the autumn and the roots in their second year.

ROSA

Botanical name: Rosa species
Part(s) used: Flowers, leaves and hips
Description: Symbolizing love and rightly named 'Queen of the Flowers' by Sappho, the rose is the most treasured of all plants, its beauty and fragrance, apart from its cosmetic, culinary or medicinal qualities, giving it pride of place. Hundreds, even thousands of rose varieties are now cultivated, new varieties being offered annually, though the old damask rose, *Rosa damascena*, apothecary's or provins rose, *Rosa gallica officinalis*, and the dog rose, *Rosa canina* – so named because it was thought to cure the bite of rabid dogs – were and still are grown for their valuable medicinal properties.

The word rose comes from the Greek for red, *rodon*. The brilliant velvety petals would be scattered at various festivals such as on the feast of Flora. The Romans even strewed the floors of their villas with the fragrant petals and, as with violets, would fashion them into wreaths and wear them at banquets in the hope that it would prevent them from becoming drunk. They made a conserve of the petals and dusted themselves with rose powder, distilled the oil and annointed themselves with it, and burnt rose pastils to sweeten the atmosphere. On feast days this fragrant and colourful symbol of mirth and romance would decorate the temples and images of the gods Bacchus, Venus and Cupid.

Rose-water was first made in the tenth century by Avicenna and the oil or otto of roses, in Persia in the seventeenth century. According to legend the discovery of the oil content in roses was made by the Mogul emperor Djihanguyr and his bride, Princess Nour-Djihan. They noticed that the canal encircling the garden that had been filled with rose-water was covered with a film of deliciously sweet-scented oil. Isolating the oil involves a complicated process but rose-water can be made with ease.

Dog rose

Rose-water
Fill a saucepan with strongly scented red rose petals and cover with water and boil. Leave to infuse and cool making sure that the pan is tightly covered and then strain. The resulting rose-water when simmered with 2oz (50g/4tbs) of sugar will give off a delightful fragrance.

A fact that should be more widely known is that the hips of the dog rose are twenty times richer in vitamin C than oranges, hence rose-hip syrup being given to babies. This was discovered during the Second World War when oranges and other sweet and palatable sources of the vitamin were not available. An infusion of the same rose hips was also thought to strengthen the brain as well as the heart and considered a tonic to the whole system. A decoction of rose petals can be used to treat conjunctivitis, while a decoction of hips has been employed as a remedy for kidney and gall-bladder complaints. Rose honey, made with an infusion of rose petals blended with honey, will soothe a sore throat and, used by aromatherapists, the oil has a reputation for dispersing post-natal blues and lovesickness.

Bowls of pot-pourri are always a welcome sight in the house, either fresh or dried. They were an indispensable medicinal and culinary ingredient of the lady's still room. The hips would be made into a nourishing jelly and the petals crystallized or used to make the following:

Rose-petal cream
Petals of 2 large red roses
Dash of lemon juice
1tbs of vanilla sugar
4tbs (56ml/¼cup) of single cream
1pt (600ml/2½cups) of double cream

Blend the single cream with the rose petals and then whisk in the sugar, lemon and double cream.

A rose was even found hanging over the dining table of private houses (a forerunner of the ceiling rose) to symbolize the fact that all conversation carried out beneath it would be private – *sub rosa*.

Cultivation: The above mentioned are wild shrubs and can be grown from cuttings or grafts. Species roses can be grown from seed though the process is a long one. Most prefer a sunny position and well-manured soil.

Harvest: Gather the petals when the dew has dried and before the bloom is full blown and use fresh or dry. Gather the leaves when they are young and tender and the hips after the first frost.

33

Rosa Aimée Vibert

ROSEMARY

Botanical name: Rosmarinus officinalis
Alternative common name(s): Romero
Part(s) used: Leaves
Description: No collection of herbs would be complete without a rosemary bush. The pale to deep blue flowers rise in clusters from the stem and base of the needle-like leaves which are dark green above and powdery white beneath. Roughly 1in (2.5cm) in length, leathery and wonderfully fragrant these are covered with a layer of volatile oil which prevents them from losing moisture in the heat. Rosemary is a plant of the warm Mediterranean regions, *Rosmarinus* meaning 'dew of the sea'. A delightful reminder of azure blue skies and the warm pungent scent of the maquis or scrub of this region; rosemary produces stronger scent when grown in the damp climate of the British Isles.

Rosemary has important medicinal, culinary and cosmetic value. It is not known when it was first introduced to this country, but there is mention of it in the Saxon *Leech Book of Bald* which dated from AD 900. A revered ceremonial herb symbolizing remembrance, friendship and fidelity, it was thrown into or placed on graves and presented to those that grieved. It was also woven into a bride's wreath, used to decorate the church and was presented, gilded or tied with ribbons, to the bridesmaids and guests. The floor of the church was strewn with it at Christmas and, as a poor man's incense, was burnt in place of the real thing. There are many legends surrounding rosemary but perhaps the best known is that it will never grow higher than Christ and, having outlived the thirty-three years of Our Lord's life, will grow only outwards rather than upwards. Another is that the flowers were originally white, only changing to blue when Mary, on the flight from Egypt, threw her blue cloak over a bush, changing its colour at the same time as giving it its distinctive fragrance. Sprigs of rosemary used to be worn to avert the evil eye and in the sixteenth and seventeenth centuries it was used to adorn the central arbour of mazes, was clipped into topiary and was as valued on festival days as holly is at Christmas today.

For Sir Thomas More, whose garden was lavishly planted with rosemary, and Shakespeare's Ophelia, the herb symbolized remembrance – it was frequently used to cure forgetfulness. Placed under a bed it was believed to ward off nightmares and, appropriately for it has antiseptic qualities, it was burnt in a sick room to disinfect and freshen the atmosphere. It would also be included in posies that were carried to guard against infectious diseases. Only take rosemary internally for a few days at a time. It is inadvisable in pregnancy. The oil should be used externally only. Smoothed on the brow it will help soothe a headache or held under the nose will revive those that feel faint. A lotion dabbed beneath the eyes will reduce puffiness and rosemary tea will stimulate the appetite and circulation and allay the symptoms of indigestion.

A much valued cosmetic herb, it does wonders for the hair. Used in the form of a rinse or shampoo it will improve the general condition and, in particular, the colour of dark shades. Make a strong decoction of the dried leaves and add it to the rinsing water or a home-made soapwort shampoo. The major ingredient of that most famous of old-fashioned beauty aids, Hungary Water, it was much in demand in the fourteenth and fifteenth centuries. The recipe for this was given to Queen Elizabeth of Hungary in 1370 by a hermit and still exists in the imperial library in Vienna.

Rosemary is a very strong herb and it should be used with discretion in the kitchen as its flavour can overwhelm all others. It is also best added at the beginning of any cooking process rather than at the end. Excellent with lamb and chicken it was and still is used to flavour certain wines and as a marinade for meat before it is cooked. The following marinade recipe can make a dull cut of meat exciting and flavoursome:

3 chopped shallots
2 crushed cloves of garlic
5 freshly ground peppercorns
Salt
1tbs of freshly stripped rosemary leaves
1 bayleaf and chopped parsley stalks

Rosemary

Add all the ingredients to ½pt (280ml/1¼cups) of olive oil and pour over the meat and leave for at least 5 hours.

Cultivation: Sow seed in trays in early spring or take cuttings of non-flowering shoots. The plant can also be layered in early summer. Preferring a well-drained soil it is most successfully grown set against a sunny wall and sheltered from the cold winds.

Harvest: Gather the leaves when the flowers are in bud and dry.

RUE

Botanical name: Ruta graveolens
Alternative common name(s): Herb of grace, herbygrass
Part(s) used: Leaves
Description: Introduced to this country by the Romans, this small, shrub-like hardy evergreen is a native of southern Europe. Despite its rank, repellent smell, its distinctive blue-green foliage and tiny pale yellow flowers make it an excellent garden plant, especially in its variegated form. A perennial growing to about 3ft (approximately 1m) high, it has woody stems, deeply divided foliage that has a bloom to it, sulphur-yellow flowers with cupped petals and a bitter taste.

The name *Ruta* comes from the Greek word *reuo*, to set free, and as a medicinal herb rue can be used as a remedy for a delayed menstruation as long as pregnancy is ruled out. It will also expel worms and calm those suffering from hysteria. The Romans believed in its power to improve the eyesight and even bestow second sight on those that took it regularly.

Herbalists through the ages have extolled its power as an antidote to 'dangerous medicines or deadly poisons'. The mid-eighteenth century saw the height of its popularity as it was considered, along with wormwood, the herb that could protect all those who carried it against the plague, a new outbreak having then been rumoured. All stocks were sold out. The floors of law courts would be strewn with it to protect the court officials from being infected by gaol fever and it was always included in the nosegays carried by a judge. Sprigs of it were used to sprinkle holy water before a Mass, hence its common name herb of grace. It was also thought to preserve chastity. Perhaps one of its strangest uses was in connection with guns. To guarantee the accuracy of a shot, flints were first boiled in a solution of rue and vervain.

Despite its bitter flavour it can be used in moderation in salads, though even John Evelyn who wrote so enthusiastically about the making of 'sallets' in the eighteenth century, did not recommend it very highly. It can be eaten fresh in sandwiches but an infusion of the leaves is probably the most palatable way of using the herb, though this should be taken in great moderation and certainly not by women who are pregnant. 1tsp of the chopped herb to 1pt (600ml/2½cups) of boiling water is recommended, the dosage being 3 wine-glass measures a day. Taken internally it will cool a fever, stimulate the appetite and soothe a troublesome stomach. Used externally as an eye bath, it might not dramatically improve the sight, but is a remedy for troublesome eyes.

Cultivation: It likes a well-drained soil and a sheltered, sunny position. Sow seed in trays in early spring and then transplant or take stem cuttings in the summer. Seed of the variegated rue has the unusual distinction of always coming true. It can have an evil effect on some of its neighbours, causing them to die inexplicably.

Harvest: Being an evergreen the herb can be gathered at any time, but is best picked before it flowers. The top-most, young shoots are the most valuable.

SAGE

Botanical name: Salvia officinalis
Alternative common name(s): Sawge, garden sage, red sage
Part(s) used: Leaves
Description: There is an old English proverb:

> He that would live for aye,
> Must eat Sage in May.

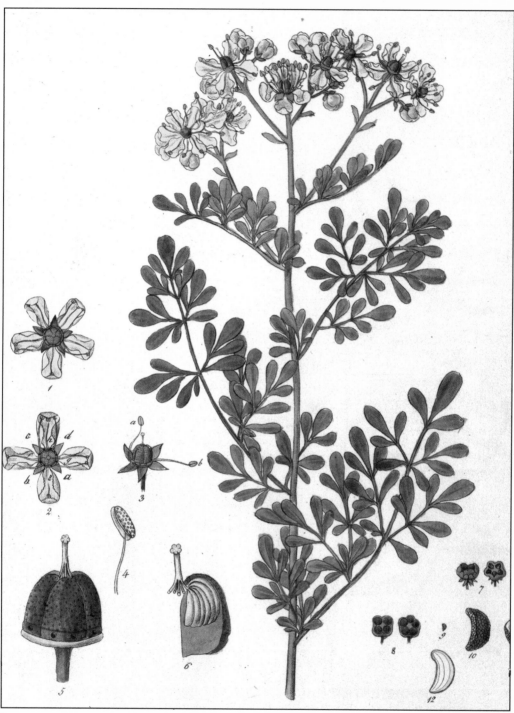

Rue

Sage certainly was and is one of the most precious of medicinal herbs. Its very name is derived from the Latin word to save, *salvare*, but the proverb's boast of it offering everlasting life is perhaps going too far. Sage is a member of a vast family of shrubs, sub shrubs, annuals and perennials; it is a native of the Mediterranean regions. *Salvia officinalis*, the true medicinal and culinary herb, grows between 1-2ft (30-60cm) high, has a woody base and violet-blue flowers borne on terminal spikes from early summer to autumn. The leaves are oblong, velvety and grey-green. These sometimes have a hang dog, tired look to them but this does not seem to affect their strong warm flavour and scent that has a distinctive oily quality.

Considered a sacred herb by the Greeks and Romans who dedicated it to Zeus and Jupiter, it symbolized domestic virtue, was thought to be a cure for sterility and a preserver, as well as giver, of life. Introduced to this country in the sixteenth century, sage butter became an important church fasting dish and sage tea widely drunk – so delicious did the Chinese find it that they exchanged it with Dutch travellers for their own more subtle 'China' tea.

It should be treated with respect in the kitchen and always given the upper hand, as, like rosemary, its flavour is very strong and drowns all others. Due to its ability to make fatty foods more digestible it is an ideal accompaniment to meats such as pork, chicken, duck and goose. Popular in stuffings, it is also used in terrines, pates and sausages. A stuffing that has an excellent flavour as well as a varied texture is composed of the following ingredients:

1 medium onion
8 sage leaves
5oz (150g) of breadcrumbs
3oz (75g) of dried apricots
2oz (50g) of raisins (soaked with the apricots for several hours)
2oz (50g) of pine nuts
2oz (50g) of butter
1 egg yolk
1 clove of garlic, crushed
Salt and pepper

Finely chop all the ingredients and mix together with cooked chicken, duck or goose liver.

Sage tea is a remedy for many ills, from hot flushes, to sore throats, colds, fevers, depression, nervous tension and indigestion. An infusion of dried or fresh leaves sweetened with honey and flavoured with the zest of a lemon, will reduce the unwanted milk of nursing mothers and help those suffering from liver or respiratory tract problems. Do not take it for more than a few days at a time, an 'overdose' can have a toxic effect. An ointment made by melting ½lb (225g) of lard with 2tbs of chopped sage leaves, brought to the boil, strained through muslin and poured into screw-topped containers will, when rubbed on the affected part, soothe rheumatism and stiffness.

As a cosmetic herb it is good for the scalp and hair as well as the complexion, helping, in a face-pack form, to close open pores. Clary sage, *Salvia sclarea* var *turkestanica*, whose large pink and pale violet flowers last well into autumn, also has its uses. An infusion of the seeds, being rich in mucilage, will make a remedial eye bath, hence the name clary or clear eye.

There is not space enough to list all the varieties of *Salvia* but the following all make rewarding garden plants. Two variegated varieties are golden sage, *Salvia officinalis* 'Icterina' and the tricolour sage, *Salvia officinalis* 'Tricolor' with its red, cream and green foliage. These need watching as they are apt to revert and, as they do not bear flowers, can be grown from cuttings or layers only. Purple sage, *Salvia officinalis* 'Purpurascens', has wine-red purplish foliage that can be used to flatter more flamboyant subjects. Pale pink and purple, lily-flowered, tulips and golden marjoram look superb when grown in tandem with purple sage. Pineapple sage, *Salvia elegans* formerly *Salvia rutilans*, has an uncannily strong scent of the exotic fruit. The hardy annual, *Salvia patens*, bears exquisite azure blue flowers in late summer and can be treated as a short-lived perennial in sheltered gardens.

Cultivation: The shrubs are apt to get leggy and need renewing every few years. Grow from seed sown in trays, or propagate by layering or from taking cuttings in spring and summer. When replacing a sage past its best, be sure to place it in a different position to achieve good results. Sage prefers dry, chalky soil and a sunny position.

Harvest: Cut the leaves in spring before the plant flowers and, if not used when fresh, dry or freeze.

SOAPWORT

Botanical name: Saponaria officinalis
Alternative common name(s): Bouncing bet, bruisewort, fuller's herb, latherwort, soapwort, sweet Betty
Part(s) used: Leaves and roots
Description: A native of central and southern Europe, this perennial herb makes an attractive herbaceous border plant, but it must be watched for it is highly invasive. The pale pink star-like flowers are borne in lax terminal clusters on red-tinged stems in July and August, and the leaves are oval and pale green.

As its name suggests this herb is valued above all others as a substitute for soap. Excellent for cleaning wool fabric it acquired its common name fuller's herb because it was used in the fulling or thickening of cloth. The President of the Herb Society and Culpeper, Lady Meade-Featherstonhaugh, revived its use as a gentle but effective cleaning agent in the 1960s. She first experimented with cleaning some fabrics that were in her home, Uppark, in Sussex, now in the care of the National Trust and unfortunately recently severely damaged by fire. These were old and valuable and might well have been ruined if washed in modern chemical detergents. By experimenting a number of ideas were tested; eventually two processes proved to be particularly successful. Simply wipe the fabric with a decoction of the leaves and roots of soapwort, the dirt should be brushed off when dry. Alternatively the fabric was spread on the lawns overnight to absorb the dew and then plunged into a bath filled with a soapwort solution. This astringent green solution (the lather was produced by the saponin content) was rinsed out with ease, the whole process resulting in cloth with revitalized colour and reconditioned fibres. Thanks to the success of the experiments undertaken at

Uppark, precious fabrics and tapestries that would otherwise have been left to rot, have been saved and rejuvenated.

Soapwort solution
Crush 1oz (28g/2tbs) of the dried root that has been soaked for several hours and place in a pan with 2pt (1120ml/5cups) of water. Bring to the boil and simmer for half an hour, cool and strain. The same solution can be made by substituting the root with five handfuls of the stems and leaves.

A shampoo can be made from the herb which, when mixed with a strong infusion of another herb such as rosemary or nettle, will soften and add shine to the hair.

Soapwort shampoo
Place three handfuls of soapwort and ½pt (280ml/1¼cups) of mineral or distilled water in a cooking pan. Bring to the boil and simmer for ten minutes. When cool, strain and add to an infusion of the other herb and bottle.

As a medicinal herb soapwort should only be used under professional supervision and should never be taken internally or made into a home-made remedy. At one time it was considered an effective cure for venereal diseases that had failed to respond to mercury. It was also prescribed for itchy skin complaints such as eczema and as a treatment for respiratory problems.

Cultivation: Sow seed where it is to grow, though it is best propagated from cuttings or by dividing the roots during the growing season. It likes a well-drained but damp and rich soil and a sunny position. Be sure to give it plenty of space as its creeping, rhizome-type roots spread far and wide.

Harvest: Pick the leaves in the summer before the plant comes into flower and dry. The roots can be gathered in the autumn and dried.

SORREL

Botanical name: Rumex acetosa
Alternative common name(s): Green sauce, sour sauce

Part(s) used: Leaves

Description: A member of the dock family and a native plant, *Rumex acetosa* is a hardy perennial that grows to about 2ft (60cm) high. Its leaves are very similar to those of the dock as are the spikes of its insignificant green and terracotta flowers. A few plants rather than a whole row is all that need be grown in the herb or vegetable garden, as only a handful of leaves is ever required. Their most common use is culinary, as sorrel gives a dish a distinctive acidic, lemony, flavour. Parkinson said of it in his *Paradisi in sole Paradisus terrestris* (1629):

Sorrell is much used in sauces both for the whole
        and the sicke … procuring unto them an
appetitie unto meate when their spirits are almost
spent with their furious and fiery fits, and is also
of a pleasant relish for the whole in quickening
up a dull stomacke that is over-loaden with every
                daies plenty of dishes.

A sauce made of sorrel, vinegar and sugar used to be served with cold meat and can be offered instead of apple sauce as an accompaniment to fatty meats such as roast pork. A purée of sorrel goes particularly well with roast duck. Fresh leaves, finely chopped, will add a tang to stuffings for fish and meat, lend a zip to an otherwise bland egg dish or, according to John Evelyn 'a quickness to a salad that it should never be left out'.

One of the most popular and delicious ways to eat sorrel is as a soup and those unfamiliar with the flavour are always intrigued by the distinctive taste.

Sorrel soup
1 medium onion
2 cloves of garlic
1 large potato
3 handfuls of sorrel
3 handfuls of spinach
2pt (1120ml/5cups) of good chicken stock
2oz (50g) of butter
Salt and pepper
Small carton (5floz/½cup) of single cream

Cook the onion in the butter and crushed garlic, then add the peeled and chopped potatoes, spinach and sorrel and cook for ten minutes before adding the stock. When the ingredients are cooked through, blend and season. Eat hot or cold and serve garnished with a tablespoon of cream.

Because the herb contains oxalic acid those suffering from rheumatism or gout, asthma, kidney or bladder complaints or renal colic, should not eat it if they wish to avoid irritating their condition. A decoction of the leaves can be taken to reduce a fever and to soothe eczema, acne and herpes while an infusion can be taken as a laxative. The leaves eaten before a meal are said to stimulate the appetite and a warm poultice of the cooked herb is effective in raising a head on an abscess or boil.

Sorrel produces a strong yellow and green dye and should be cherished by those who own or collect old embroidered or laced linen for it will fade or completely eradicate the mark if rubbed on to a brown rust spot before washing.

Cultivation: Sow seed where it is to grow and propagate by root division in the spring. It likes a rich, lime-free, moist soil and partial shade.

Harvest: Pick the leaves before they become too tough and use fresh or frozen. The flower stalks should be cut back if a constant supply of fresh and tender leaves is required.

SOUTHERNWOOD

Botanical name: *Artemisia abrotanum*

Alternative common name(s): Boy's love, lad's love, old man's tree

Part(s) used: Herb

Description: No herb garden would be complete without this deliciously scented perennial. Its usefulness matches its looks, the soft feathery grey-green leaves forming a bush-shaped plant about 4ft (1.2m) high. A native of southern Europe it is seldom warm enough in this country for it to be prompted into producing a crop of small, yellow-white flowers. When the settlers took it to America it failed to weather the bitter cold but after much coaxing it flourished and ultimately became naturalized in the New World. The vogue for grey, white and silver

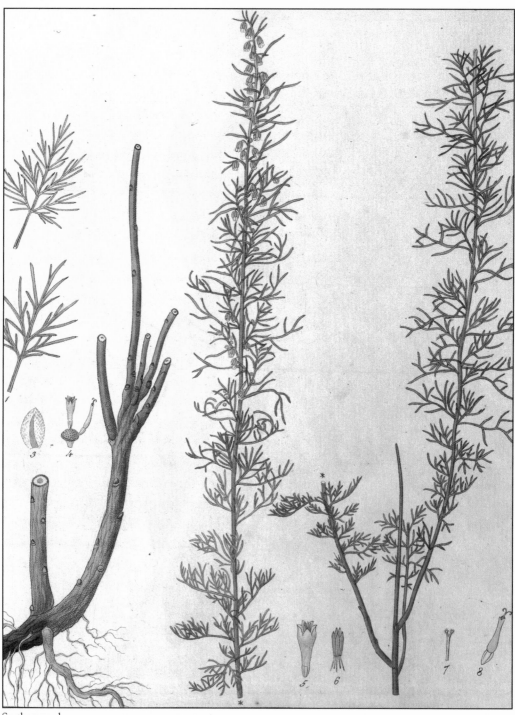

Southernwood

borders and gardens has guaranteed its place in the ornamental garden as well as the herb garden, the finely toothed silver foliage acting as a foil to colourful plants.

Southernwood is a favourite with flower arrangers and it also produces a good yellow dye. Its sweet lemony scent is one of its most attractive qualities – it is not difficult to understand why it was in such demand as a strewing herb. The ability to repel insects further recommends it. The French, always supremely practical, call it *garde robe* for a bunch hung in a wardrobe or placed in a drawer will protect clothing from moth attack. Even bees veer away from it and as a companion plant in the vegetable and fruit garden it is an excellent deterrent against cabbage white butterfly and also the fruit moth.

An antiseptic, it was thought with good reason in the past, that it would ward off infection, fear of catching the plague being a major preoccupation. Like rue it was also set around a prisoner in the dock, to protect those in the court from catching gaol fever.

An infusion of the fresh leaves will vitalize dull hair and cure dandruff and Culpeper even recommended it as a treatment for hair loss: 'The ashes mingled with old salad oil, helps those that are bald, causing the hair to grow again on the head or beard'.

The Greeks and Romans treated it as an aphrodisiac, placing it beneath their mattresses; they also believed that it had magic properties. More recently, country folk would allow it to grow lanky and twine it around the palings surrounding their cottage gardens. In the ninth century the herbalist Walafred Strabo wrote 'Southernwood of the hair-like leaves cures fevers and wounds: it has well-nigh as many virtues as leaves'. The dried and powdered herb mixed with treacle would be given to children to rid them of worms and an infusion or poultice of the dried or fresh herb was used as an antiseptic wash or placed on a wound.

Cultivation: As it rarely flowers it cannot be grown from seed but should be propagated by green cuttings taken in summer or woody cuttings taken in autumn. These should be at least 8in (20.5cm) long, the leaves having been stripped off the main part. Place in a bed or pot of damp sand, allowing only the uppermost part of the cutting to appear above the surface. Plants like a light soil and a sunny position and, to preserve their bush-like shape, should be pruned hard back in spring.

Harvest: Cut the stems in July and August and hang up in bunches to dry. When the leaves are thoroughly dried, gently strip off and store.

SUMMER SAVORY

Botanical name: Satureja hortensis
Alternative common name(s): Garden savory
Part(s) used: Herb
Description: Growing to about 1ft 8in (50cm) high, this small bush-like hardy annual resembles, though is taller than, its fellow Mediterranean herb, thyme. It has thin, oblong green leaves with spikes of pale lavender, pink or white flowers, the whole plant having a sweet aroma and flavour that is delicate and spicy.

First cultivated in the ninth century it was originally an Italian garden herb. It was introduced to this country in the early sixteenth century and was then taken to the New World by the first English settlers. Summer savory was the strongest culinary herb in use (until new species were brought from the East Indies) and it was also considered an aphrodisiac. Once known as the 'herb of love' it was always associated with satyrs, hence the name *Satureja*, and monks were forbidden to grow it in their gardens. It is still used as an aphrodisiac, the dried and powdered leaves being sprinkled on food or a decoction of savory and fenugreek rubbed into the base of the spine.

Perhaps its greatest claim to fame as a medicinal herb is due to its extraordinary ability to combat flatulence. If savory is cooked along with Jerusalem artichokes, dried beans, fresh broad beans or added to a cucumber salad it will prevent any unpleasant effects. The cooking smells of sprouts and cauliflowers can also be dispelled by adding savory to the boiling water.

Cultivation: It likes a rich, well-drained soil and a sunny position. Sow the seed in April. Savory

Satureia

ica et tremore tanta fu

p contritione et amore

opofito et humilitate fi

xdit faluti amine mee.

cht quefo illius domming

e non folum fufapur fa

tuum fz et effectum facu

. Omntiffime domme df

ht fufapur corpus Vm

tu domm noftri refu

od traxit df uurgine na

corpori fuo miftico meu

rporay ac inter fantta

iembra falubriter comi

i. O pater amantiffime

t mmchi dilectum filium

quem nunc quidem Ve

Sarriete.

Summer savory

is an ideal candidate for a pot or window-box planted with herbs.

Harvest: Gather when the plant is in flower, pulling the whole plant and hanging it up to dry.

WINTER SAVORY

Botanical name: Satureja montana
Alternative common name(s): Mountain savory
Part(s) used: Herb
Description: Very aromatic and with a much stronger, harsher flavour than summer savory. It makes a compact, small, evergreen bush. A perennial, it has oblong but smaller and tougher leaves than those of the annual, and bears pink or lilac flowers in late summer and early autumn. Winter savory is an important ingredient of salami and other preserved meats; it is also used in bouquet garni and to flavour soups, stews or add spice to a vinaigrette dressing.

A useful plant in the garden, in Tudor times it frequently traced the pattern of a knot garden or marked out a dwarf shrub maze. As a medicinal herb it is a carminative, digestive and stimulant (the latter property quite possibly giving the herb its reputation as an aphrodisiac). It is a remedy for diarrhoea and is also prescribed as a purgative and eradicator of worms. Culpeper wrote that:

It culteth rough flegm in the chest and lungs,
and helpeth to expectorate more easily. It
quencheth the dull spirits in the lethargy, the
juice thereof being snuffed or cart up into the
nostrils. The juice dropped into the Eyes cleareth
a dull sight, if it proceed of thin cold humars
distilling from the brain. The juice heated in a
little oil of Roses, and dropped into the ears
easeth them of the noise and singing in them,
and of deafness also. Outward applied with white
flour in manner of a poultice, it giveth ease to the
sciatica and palsied members, heating and
warming them and taking away their pains.

To this long list he also added colic and asthma which must mark savory as an extraordinarily versatile medicinal herb. A final recommenda-

tion is that the leaves of both kinds can be crushed to soothe bee and wasp stings.

Cultivation: It thrives on poor, limey soil and relishes a sunny position. Grow from seed sown in April, by layering or root division. Cuttings can be taken in spring, summer or autumn. The plant is best replaced every three years and should be cut back each autumn. Though a perennial it is not always hardy and in a harsh climate should be grown as an annual.

Harvest: Gather the leaves during the summer and use fresh or frozen. They are apt to be tough if dried.

SWEET CICELY

Botanical name: Myrrhis odorata
Alternative common name(s): British myrrh, anise, great chervil, sweet chervil, the Roman plant, shepherd's needle, sweet bracken, sweet fern
Part(s) used: Leaves, roots and seeds
Description: It seems appropriate that a herb with such a charming name should indeed be sweet, and can even be used in place of sugar when cooking sharp fruits such as damsons and rhubarb. Consequently it is a friend to those who suffer from diabetes or are trying to lose weight. It is thought to have been introduced from Europe but has grown wild in this country for so long that it is frequently mistaken for a native.

The Latin name *Myrrhis odorata* comes from the Greek for perfume and the plant was later dedicated to St Cecilia, becoming shortened on occasion to the delightful name of Sweet Cis. The Romans would plant it in their garden wherever they went, partly to eat but also to attract bees; in the seventeenth century the seed was finely ground and mixed with bees wax to make a furniture polish.

The fresh green foliage is wonderfully decorative, being feathery and fern-like, and the creamy white flowers are borne on umbels in early summer. Growing to a considerable size, it can reach 5ft (1.5m) high and spread 3ft (90cm) wide which makes it a handsome perennial border plant that could be used to flatter more flamboyant neighbours.

The fruit it produces is ridged and unusually long, at first a fresh green but gradually turning a brownish black as they ripen. These taste strongly of anise and when young can be used in salads or when ripe as a spice in place of cloves. The sweet-tasting leaves also have the flavour of anise and mingled with lovage and then finely chopped add a delicious flavour to scrambled eggs or an omelette. But it is the long tapering root that has the strongest flavour. Grated raw it will add zest to a salad and sliced and cooked can be eaten as a vegetable which Gerard found to be 'very good for old people that are dull and without courage; it rejoiceth and comforteth the heart and increaseth their lust and strength'.

As a medicinal herb chewing the seeds will relieve mild indigestion. An infusion of the crushed seeds or leaves is a remedy for flatulence and will also stimulate the appetite and clear the bronchial tubes. Professional herbalists have used it to treat anaemia and a decoction of the root makes an effective antiseptic. It was once thought to be an excellent remedy for those who had been bitten by a mad dog or viper; certainly the old herbalists held it in high esteem due to it being 'so harmless you cannot use it amiss'.

Cultivation: Take root cuttings in spring or sow seed in the autumn. The seed needs exposure to the cold before it germinates, so if sown in the spring the tray should be placed in a cold fridge for at least ten days. Once established the plant will self sow with ease. It likes a well-drained, fertile, acid soil and prefers a shady position.

Harvest: The root should be dug up in the autumn and dried or used fresh and the leaves used fresh or picked for drying in spring and summer.

SWEET VIOLET

Botanical name: Viola odorata
Alternative common name(s): Sweet scented violet
Part(s) used: Leaves and flowers
Description: The sweet violet is one of our most charming native plants and lifts the spirits early in the year as it flowers from February to April and sometimes in September. It has the distinction of having been one of the first plants to be grown, not for its practical uses, but for its intrinsic beauty. Growing from rhizomes that spread by means of runners it has mid-green, heart-shaped leaves and flowers that are various shades of purple or white.

It was much beloved by the Greeks, Romans and Persians who used it as a cosmetic, perfume,

Dog violet

medicinal herb and flavouring agent. It flavoured their wine, was wound into garlands which they wore to ward off a hangover, was painted on their eyelids and taken to cure a headache and induce sleep. It was dedicated to Aphrodite whose son Priapus was the god of fertility and in medieval times the violet symbolized the humility of Our Lord. For centuries it has been mixed with orris root to make a perfume, the sweet scent of 'Devon Violets' being used to enhance all sorts of products from writing paper to soap.

The leaves and delicate flowers can be eaten fresh in salads or dried and crystallized and used to decorate cakes and puddings. Pick the flower heads and wash and drain, then dip them in a solution of rose-water and gum arabic. Powder with castor sugar and place on a non-stick baking sheet and put in a very cool oven until dry. A decoction of the flowers can be made that will relieve a headache and soothe a feverish cold, while a syrup can be taken to treat chesty colds. A poultice of the freshly crushed, ovate, leaves will reduce swellings and treat cracked nipples.

Cultivation: Sow in the autumn and overwinter as the seeds need low temperatures to break their dormancy. Do not be disappointed if the results are poor as germination can be erratic. It can also be propagated by offsets being taken in autumn or early spring and planted in equal quantities of peat and sand. Violets prefer a semi-shaded, moist and slightly acidic soil and, once established, will spread.

Harvest: Gather the flowers and leaves in the summer and use fresh or dry.

TANSY

Botanical name: Tanacetum vulgare
Alternative common name(s): Batchelor's buttons, bitter buttons
Part(s) used: Leaves and flowers
Description: Tansy is a native plant that grows to about 3ft (90cm) high, its erect stems bearing finely toothed and divided, feathery leaves. Atop the tall stems are flat umbels of golden yellow, button-like flowers from mid to late summer,

hence the common name batchelor's and bitter buttons. Dedicated to the Virgin Mary it was placed, as a symbol of immortality, in coffins and used in the embalming process, the Greek word *athanaton*, from which comes *Tanacetum*, meaning 'undying'.

Tansy was one of the many herbs that were taken by the settlers to the New World and it became naturalized so rapidly there that it now decorates the lanes and hedgerows of New England and Pennsylvania. In the Middle Ages it was chiefly used as a strewing herb for it not only sweetened the otherwise fetid and unhygienic atmosphere, but also served to keep pests at bay. When the plague was raging through the land it was also strewn in public places such as law courts and churches. The leaves would be rubbed on the surface of far from fresh meat and a bunch of tansy hung up in the larder to keep the flies away – an economical and practical tip well worth taking note of today.

Though not popular as a culinary herb due to its bitter taste it was an important ingredient of Lenten fare, the bitterness of tansy cakes and pancakes acting as a reminder to those that ate them of Christ's suffering. The finely chopped leaves imparted not only this bitter flavour but a strong yellow colour. Tansy taken at this time was not only a religious ritual but also considered a tonic to the system that had endured the leaden winter diet and the customary salt and fish of the Lenten period. The cakes would also be awarded to the victors of what was known as the Easter Games when every member of the congregation, from the bishop to the poorest peasant, played handball. Recipes for cakes, many of which date from the fifteenth and sixteenth centuries, would now be considered too extravagant as the ingredients frequently included vast quantities of almonds, brandy, cream and eggs.

Tansy can be toxic if taken in large doses, consequently it is not greatly used in medicine and should only be taken when administered by a professional herbalist and should certainly never be prescribed to pregnant women: being an emmenagogue, it provokes menstruation which can lead to premature birth. A decoction of the leaves was used to treat scabies and an infusion,

Tansy

taken on rising and going to bed, would rid children of worms. Because it promotes perspiration it is a good fever herb and a poultice of the leaves will soothe varicose veins and sprains.

Tansy is a popular dye plant for its leaves produce a good golden yellow solution, but they must be picked before the plant comes into flower. It is an attractive border plant but must be given plenty of room to spread, its white runners being well able to crawl a couple of feet (up to a metre) in a season. It also seeds itself freely. One of its main advantages in the ornamental garden is that it flowers late and long – its heads of 'buttons' will only be turned black by a heavy frost. Flower arrangers find its straight, rigid stems easy to handle and because the buttons retain their colour when dried, it is as useful in fresh summer arrangements as in dried winter creations.

Cultivation: Tansy will thrive almost anywhere but abhors a permanently wet position. Its preference is for a moist loam or sand. It can be grown from seed or by root division in spring or autumn.

Harvest: Gather the leaves in spring and summer and dry. The flowers should be cut and hung up to dry just before they reach their peak.

TARRAGON

Botanical name: Artemisia dracunculus
Alternative common name(s): French tarragon, little dragon, mugwort
Part(s) used: Leaves
Description: A native of southern Europe, tarragon was certainly well established in this country by Tudor times and no garden was considered 'well dressed' without it. Growing to 2ft (60cm) high with thin stems bearing 2in- (5cm-) long, narrow, leaves, it is strongly aromatic. The flavour has a perfumed quality but is also peppery and reminiscent of liquorice and camphor. The yellow flowers are very insignificant, seldom open and never produce seed. Unless seen side by side it is easy to mistake the French tarragon for the Russian, *Artemisia dracunculoides*, which has a slightly paler green foliage, grows higher and

spreads wider and has an inferior scent and flavour. The Russian variety is frequently passed off as the French in nurseries so special care should be taken when buying a plant – tasting the flavour is a sure test.

It acquired its Latin name *dracunculus* because of its often invasive, coiling white root that was thought to resemble a dragon's tail. These white whippy roots were also instrumental in bestowing upon it a reputation for curing the effects of snake and dog bites, as well as toothache. Although essentially a culinary herb, John Evelyn thought that 'Tis high cordial and friendly to the head, heart and Liver'. An infusion of the dried leaves will soothe an unhappy digestion, treat wind, nausea and rheumatic pain. It is cooling and a carminative and can also be used as a diuretic, a treatment for catarrh and will help purify the blood. The leaves chewed raw will also eradicate, for a short time at least, halitosis.

Tarragon ranks very high in the league table of culinary herbs, especially as an accompaniment to fish, poultry and salads. It is a traditional ingredient of béarnaise and tartare sauce and the old-fashioned ravigote sauce which can be served to cheer up an otherwise dull plate of fish, beef, chicken or vegetables.

Ravigote sauce
Make a vinaigrette with 3tbs (42ml/¼cup) of wine vinegar and 8tbs (140ml/½cup) of olive oil and add:
1tsp of finely chopped onion
1tsp of mustard powder
1tsp of chopped capers
2tbs of chopped tarragon
1tbs of chopped parsley
1 dessert-spoon (2tsp) of castor sugar

Blend all the ingredients together

Another very simple sauce that is an unusual and tasty accompaniment to eggs and lightly cooked vegetables such as courgettes or carrots is tarragon cream. Add to ½pt (10fl oz) of double cream 1tbs of chopped fresh tarragon and season. Fresh tarragon leaves add a delicious tang to a salad and the ever-popular recipe for tarragon chicken.

Tarragon chicken
1 fresh chicken
Bunch of tarragon
3oz (75g/1cup) of butter
Salt, pepper and lemon
2 egg yolks
½pt (10fl oz) of cream

Rub the chicken with lemon and put the butter blended with salt, pepper and half the tarragon inside the bird. Poach until cooked and leave to cool. Whip the cream, remainder of the chopped tarragon and egg yolks together and having added half the cooking juices, blend over a low heat with the cream mixture until it thickens. Pour over the chicken and allow to cool before serving.

Cultivation: Tarragon is a perennial and likes a sunny position and a light soil. It can only be grown from root or stem cuttings taken in spring and should be propagated and replanted every three or four years, being placed in a different spot each time.

Harvest: Cut the stems in August before the plant has flowered and strip off the leaves and dry or freeze.

THYME

Botanical name: Thymus vulgaris
Alternative common name(s): Common thyme, garden thyme, tomillo
Part(s) used: Leaves and flowers
Description: In the Middle Ages ladies would give their knights a sprig of thyme or a hand-embroidered 'favour' that depicted a bee hovering over the herb, in the hope that it would imbue them with courage. In addition to being valued as a symbol of bravery it was also used to flavour drinks at this time, but its history is even longer than those facts would seem to suggest. Known to have been grown in ancient Babylon it was also a favourite of the Greeks who used it as a strewing and fumigatory herb. The Latin word *Thymus* comes from the Greek *thuo* which means 'to perfume'.

Wonderfully aromatic and rich in volatile oil,

it is a proven antiseptic and used to be carried by those fearful of being infected by the plague and leprosy. Charlemagne laid down that it should be planted in all herb gardens and by the sixteenth century it was well established in this country. Thyme is a hardy perennial that forms a small evergreen bush, whose short woody stalks are covered with tiny grey-green leaves. The flowers appear from May to September and are various shades of lilac and borne in whorls at the end of the stems; the root system is shallow and fibrous.

As a medicinal herb John Gerard described it as being 'profitable for such as are fearfull, melancholicke and troubled in mind'. It was certainly used by the ancients as a preventative against nightmares, to calm convulsions and soothe the nervous system. Thyme is a tonic and a stimulant and has also been prescribed for depression and lethargy and, made into a soup, was thought to cure shyness. The herb contains thymol which is effective in expelling worms from the system and is an ingredient of modern toothpastes and mouthwashes. An infusion used externally will disinfect boils, burns and cuts and taken internally can be used to treat colds and bronchial problems, as well as being an effective gargle for a sore throat.

The wild or creeping thyme, *Thymus serpyllum*, has a warm incense-like fragrance and can be used in the same way as garden thyme, both medicinally and in the kitchen, though its flavour is not as strong. Growing in the wild on

Wild thyme

dry, heath-type ground its presence, like that of lichen, is a sign that the atmosphere is clean. Parkinson was accurate when he wrote of the many different varieties 'We preserve them with all the care we can in our gardens, for the sweete and pleasant scents and varieties they yield'. The many varieties include the caraway thyme, or Corsican thyme, *Thymus herba-barona*, which is prostrate, and fast spreading and has a genuine scent of caraway; the Golden thyme, *Thymus vulgaris aureus*, the gold variegated thyme; lemon thyme, *Thymus citriodorus*; orange thyme and a collection of silver-leafed varieties such as silver posie (*Thymus vulgaris*) and silver queen (*Thymus citriodurus*), and many others. All are beloved by butterflies and even more so by bees. Hives would be rubbed with the herb and plants would be grown nearby, the flavour of thyme honey being extremely sought after. The prostrate thymes are ideal candidates for planting between paving stones, as edgers, excellent ground cover in crevices and cracks of walls and on lawns. When the plants are pressed underfoot their delicious scent is released.

Thyme is an indispensable ingredient of bouquet garni and as a culinary herb it is a good digestive, especially when mixed with cream cheeses or cooked with fatty meats. The warm pungent smell and flavour adds greatly to the enjoyment of barbecued meats, while lemon thyme adds a refreshing, citrus tang to a fish dish, cool summer drink or fruit salad.

Dried sprigs hung in a wardrobe or linen cupboard will keep moths at bay and an infusion makes an excellent hair conditioner, especially for dark shades. Used as a decoction in a bath it will refresh and soothe sufferers of skin complaints or rheumatism. The flowers and leaves, when dried, will scent the atmosphere in a pot-pourri or herb cushion.

Cultivation: Sow the seed in March or April where it is to flower and then thin. Thymes relish a sunny situation and well-drained, stony or gravelly soil. It can be propagated by stem cuttings or root division in spring, but the easiest method of increasing plants is by layering. Give the plant plenty of room, see that it is not put in the same place twice, and trim it back each year.

Harvest: Cut sprigs of the herb in the summer and hang in bunches to dry; then rub off the leaves and store. Fresh sprigs can also be preserved in olive oil.

YARROW

Botanical name: Achillea millefolium
Alternative common name(s): Bloodwort, carpenter's weed, milfoil, nose bleed, woundwort
Part(s) used: Herb

Sneezewort yarrow

Thymus Serpyllum.

Yarrow

Description: One of the most familiar of all our native herbs, yarrow is considered a weed in the garden but an attractive flower in the wild. A common sight in hedgerows, fields and lanes it can grow up to 2ft (60cm) high, has straight stalks, feathery grey-green foliage that is slightly hairy, and flat clusters of white flowers, that are frequently tinged with pink. The aroma of the plant is not particularly pleasant and the taste pungent and bitter.

As its country names reveal it has considerable medicinal qualities; the ability to staunch the flow of blood has justified its use for centuries. Achilles, a pupil of the wild old centaur of Greek mythology, Chiron, is said to have been the first to realise the herb's value and used it to treat his wounded warriors, hence the generic name *Achillea*. Greek and Roman soldiers would carry it into battle, as a readily available first-aid kit for themselves or their comrades who had sustained a profusely bleeding open wound. Plugs of the fresh leaves are adept at stopping a nosebleed, and taken internally as an infusion yarrow will check a heavy period or haemorrhage.

An infusion can also be prescribed to treat the early symptoms of a cold and release a suppressed fever by provoking perspiration. A tea made with the flowers will soothe indigestion, prevent flatulence and clear obstinate catarrh.

Being an astringent, it makes a good cosmetic herb, used alone or with others to cleanse and clear the complexion. Yarrow is excellent for an oily skin and a facial steam made of the herb will bring impurities to the surface, close open pores and stimulate the circulation. This recipe for a face pack will serve equally well:

Finely chop a handful of the fresh flowers and leaves and place them in a pan. Cover with water, bring to the boil and then simmer for 10 minutes, being careful not to allow the steam to escape. Strain the resulting warm pulp and place between muslin or gauze and lay on the face. Always cover the eyes and mouth with damp cotton wool. Relax for 10 minutes and then remove the pack and rinse the face with tepid water.

Yarrow should not be used too often as it can cause discolouration of the skin and, after experimenting on a small patch, do not use at all if you have an allergic reaction. It should only be used in small quantities internally as it has been known to cause vertigo and headaches.

Its culinary uses are limited but the finely chopped leaves can add a zest to a salad. It generally acts as a tonic to one's health and offers a degree of protection against infection. It was once used as a substitute for hops in beer and was also an ingredient of snuff, acting, most probably, as an inbuilt antidote to the powder's often harmful effects.

There are some attractive cultivated varieties of yarrow that, due to their long flowering season, are much valued garden plants. *Achillea filipendula*, with its long stalks topped by flat, tight heads of golden or lemon-yellow flowers, is a great standby and much recommended as a subject for drying. *Achillea ptarmica*, is quite different in character but no less attractive and useful in the ornamental garden. It has heads of small, button-like, white flowers that are bolder but reminiscent of gypsophila.

Cultivation: It will grow almost anywhere and seed itself freely or will spread by means of creeping roots. The seed of wild and cultivated varieties should be sown in spring, the seeds pressed gently into the compost and not covered by soil. It can also be propagated by root division.

Harvest: Collect the leaves before the plant flowers and the flowers before they are fully open.

PLANTS FOR SPECIAL SITUATIONS

Not all the herbs listed are described in detail in the A–Z Herbal section

LOW-GROWING HEDGING AND EDGING PLANTS
Catmint
Dwarf box
Curry plant
Germander
Hyssop
Lavender
Rosemary
Sage
Santolina
Southernwood

LOW-GROWING PLANTS FOR THE FRONT OF BEDS AND BETWEEN PAVING STONES
Adjuga
Chives
Feverfew
Lady's mantle
Marjoram
Parsley
Pinks
Pennyroyal
Thyme
Violets

HERBS THAT CAN BE GROWN IN LAWNS
Chamomile
Thyme

HERBS FOR POTS, WINDOW-BOXES OR TROUGHS
Basil	Nasturtium
Bay	Parsley
Chervil	Tarragon
Chives	Thyme
Lemon balm	Summer savoury
Mint	

Below
A hedge of purple sage.

Colts foot

HERBS WITH EVERGREEN FOLIAGE

Adjuga
Aloe
Bay
Chervil
Feverfew
Houseleek
Hyssop
Rosemary
Rue
Sage
Santolina
Southernwood
Thyme
Winter savoury
Wormwood

TALL-GROWING HERBS

Agrimony
Angelica
Clary sage
Dill
Elecampane
Evening primrose
Fennel
Foxglove
Lovage
Marshmallow
Mullein
Tansy

HERBS WITH VERY LARGE, VARIEGATED OR INTERESTING FOLIAGE

Aloe
Comfrey
Elecampane
Feverfew, golden
Fennel, bronze
Golden marjoram
Houseleek
Lemon balm, variegated
Pulmonaria
Rue, variegated
Sage, purple or variegated
Thyme, golden, silver or variegated

GROUND-COVERING HERBS

Adjuga
Chamomile
Ground ivy
Pennyroyal
Sweet violet

SHADE-TOLERANT HERBS

Adjuga
Evening primrose
Foxglove
Hellebore
Lady's mantle
Lily of the valley
Mint
Pennyroyal
Primrose
Pulmonaria
Solomon's seal
Sweet violet
Woodruff

Cowslip

Opposite
Golden marjoram in the ornamental garden.

Borage and variegated golden sage decorate a border.

MOISTURE-LOVING HERBS

Agrimony
Angelica
Bergamot
Comfrey
Elecampane
Iris (yellow flag)
Marshmallow
Meadowsweet
Mint
Soapwort
Sweet cicely
Sorrel

HERBS FOR DRY SITUATIONS

Chamomile
Curry plant
Fennel

Foxglove
Houseleek
Hyssop
Rosemary
Sage
Santolina
Thyme
Winter savoury

SCENTED HERBS

Bergamot
Catmint
Chamomile
Clove carnations
Curry plant
Evening primrose
Hyssop pinks
Lavender
Lemon balm
Lily of the valley
Marjoram
Meadowsweet

Thyme
Rose
Rosemary
Southernwood
Violets
Winter savoury

BEE AND BUTTERFLY HERBS

Agrimony
Anise
Basil
Bergamot
Borage
Broom
Catmint
Chamomile
Chives
Clover
Coltsfoot
Comfrey

Dandelion
Elder
Evening primrose
Fennel
Foxglove
Hyssop
Lemon balm
Lavender
Marjoram
Marshmallow
Mint
Meadowsweet
Nettle
Parsley
Pinks
Rosemary
Sage
Thyme
Yarrow

Wild geranium or herb Robert

Home-Made Herbal Products

POT-POURRI

A pot-pourri is a sweet-smelling medley of dried flowers, petals, leaves, citrus fruit peel and seeds to which has been added spices and essential oils. A fixative, such as common or sea salt, powdered orris root, gum benzoin or storax, is also needed to prevent the essential oils, and consequently the pot-pourri, from losing its fragrance when exposed to the air.

Originally used to sweeten the often fetid atmosphere of stuffy and unhygienic rooms, a bowl of this deliciously scented mixture served the same purpose as a strewing herb. It disguised unpleasant smells, repelled insects and, in some cases such as in the sick room, acted as an antiseptic.

Pot-pourri has enjoyed a huge revival of late and the natural and evocative scent of garden flowers is gradually beginning to usurp the relatively harsh scents produced by modern aerosol and other air fresheners. There are two kinds of pot-pourri, a dry and a moist. The former is easy to make and use and is consequently now the most popular of the two. A moist pot-pourri has a longer life but the length of time it takes to make and the fact that it is not a decorative, as well as a fragrant, feature, have led to its demise.

Do not slavishly follow a recipe for a pot-pourri but experiment with different ingredients until you alight upon the fragrance that best suits your personal preferences. In former times households would have had their own formulas, one that reflected the chatelaine's individual taste as well as the contents of her garden. It is fun to create a different fragrance for each season of the year. A winter mix can include the spicey scents of cinnamon or juniper and contain dried berries, fir cones, citrus peel studded with cloves, star anise, litchen or scented bark and wood shavings. While one composed of lavender, rose petals, pinks and scented geranium leaves conjures up the fresh sweetness of a summer garden.

For a dry pot-pourri gather the fresh ingre-dients when they are at their best and most fragrant. The dew should have evaporated, the day be warm and the flowers not damaged in any way. Leaves should be picked when they are young and before the plant has come into flower. Their scent is then at its strongest. Spread them out to dry on muslin, net or paper stretched over boxes or frames that allow the air to circulate freely and then cover with a sheet of foil or muslin. To preserve the colour of the ingredients dry the mixture slowly in the shade, the petals or whole flower heads should be turned every few days until they are papery. Do not be tempted to use flowers past their best or in full bloom, as their petals will have lost their scent and be apt to curl and brown at the edges. The most successful pot-pourris contain one part dried aromatic leaves to seven parts scented flower petals, but today there are no precise rules and all sorts of scented plant material can be used to good effect.

Basic recipe for dry pot-pourri

To every pint (600ml/2½ cups) of mixed dried flowers and leaves add 1tsp of mixed powdered spices (though spices such as pieces of cinnamon stick, star anise, juniper berries, etc, can be added in a non-powdered form), 1tbs of powdered orris root, this will act as a fixative, and a few drops of essential oil, no more than two kinds ever being used together.

Basic recipe for moist pot-pourri

Dry whole flowers, petals and leaves until they are leathery rather than papery. To every pint (600ml/2½cups) of dried material placed in a wide-necked jar add 1tbs of powdered orris root and 2tbs of salt. Mix thoroughly adding 1tsp of one or two essential oils. Moisten by sprinkling with brandy, rose- or orange-water. Leave for a

Opposite
Pot-pourri, herbal pillow and linen and wardrobe sachets.

110

month and always cover when the pot-pourri is not being used. Keep moist by regularly adding more brandy or scented water.

Lemon-scented dry pot-pourri with an attractive colouring

2pt (1120ml/5cups) of yellow and orange pot or African marigold petals
1pt (600ml/2½cups) of yellow rose petals
½pt (280ml/1¼cups) of blue delphinium petals
½pt (280ml/1¼cups) of blue cornflowers
½pt (280ml/1¼cups) of lemon verbena or scented geranium leaves
1tbs of chopped and dried lemon peel
1tsp of allspice
1tbs of orris root to fix the scent
4 drops of bergamot and lemon grass oil

HERB PILLOW

It is now well known that certain aromas can have a dramatic effect on our physical and emotional well-being, hence the popularity of aromatherapy. Certain herbs, such as bergamot, stimulate the system and raise the spirits, while others, such as lavender and chamomile have a soothing effect. A small cushion filled with dried herbs will add fragrance to a bedroom, the bedclothes and, if partly filled with hops, will prove soporific.

Collect and dry sweet-smelling petals and leaves of roses, lavender, lemon balm, sweet woodruff, marjoram, mint, scented geranium leaves, thyme, rosemary, lemon verbena and hops. Mix a teaspoon of spices, ground orange or lemon peel and a tablespoon of orris root and place in a screw-top jar. Place this out of the light for a couple of weeks. Before using add a few drops of one or two essential oils. Make a small white cotton cushion cover in which to put the mixture and a pretty over-cover that can be taken off and washed when necessary. Use a lightweight fabric that will allow the scent to escape from the cushion. These cushions do not stay fragrant forever and should be restocked with freshly dried plant material each year. Those that contain that well-known sleep inducing agent, hops, lose their potency after six months.

A smaller version can be made and hung in a cupboard or placed in a chest of drawers to protect clothes from moths. This sachet should be filled with dried insect repellent herbs such as rosemary, rue, southernwood, tansy, thyme and wormwood. To one pint (600ml/2½cups) of dried material add a teaspoon of ground and mixed cinnamon, nutmeg and cloves and a teaspoon of orris root. Having allowed the mixture to mature for two weeks add only a drop of essential oil before putting it into the sachets. To ensure that the sachet continues to act effectively as an insect repellent, refill every six months from an airtight jar of the mixture. This should, of course, be kept out of the light.

TUSSIE MUSSIE

Anyone who has sold a house knows that the smell that first greets a potential buyer can have a dramatic effect on their first impressions of the property. The scent of flowers, of baking or furniture polish is always seductive and welcoming and frequently conjures up memories of much-loved places that have been long forgotten. A simple and effective way of making a home smell delicious is to simmer some herbs, fruits and spices and allow their fragrance to float through the house. The herbs can then be made into muslin bags and given as gifts, though they should be carefully labelled as a muslin bag of herbs could easily be mistaken for bouquet garni and popped in a stew. Mixtures can be made up to suit individual taste, but here is one suggestion: the dried and chopped stalks and flowers of herbs such as lavender, that might otherwise have been discarded, a bay leaf, pieces of cinnamon stick, juniper berries and dried citrus peel, powdered spices, cloves and a drop or two of an essential oil such as cedarwood, sandalwood or clove.

A posy or tussie mussie of herbs is a fragrant and attractive feature as well as an acceptable gift, with a history! As far back as the Middle Ages these posies were carried to ward off pestilential smells and infections. Even today assize judges are given them to carry into court,

though the danger of catching gaol fever has happily long since passed. A sprig of rue was a traditional ingredient of the posy as it was believed to protect the carrier from disease. Advances in health and hygiene, not to mention its rather unpleasant smell, have put an end to its inclusion today. Sprigs of herbs and fresh-scented flowers and foliage should be gathered into a small bunch. One kind of leaf, possibly that of the lemon-scented geranium – or a paper doily if a period touch is required – is used to create a frill around the posy which is then tied with a ribbon. Dried flowers, sprigs of herb and drops of various essential oils carefully placed on to the soft 'eye' of the flowers add the finishing touch to the posy.

Wild roses and honeysuckle

HERBS AND COSMETICS

From time immemorial herbs have been used to enhance one's appearance. The Egyptians, Persians, Greeks and Romans knew how to extract the essential oils from plants and were adept at making perfumes. Certain herbs were used to care for the teeth, others for the hair or complexion, the various recipes being handed down and adapted from generation to generation. The following beauty aids will suit most skin types, though always test for any allergic reaction on a small area of skin before using extensively. Having made the herbal preparations yourself, you will know that they contain only natural ingredients and that no unnecessary expense has been spent on 'presentation'.

Perfumed soap shells and hearts
10oz (300g) of castile soap
8 fl oz (225ml/1cup) of rosewater or a strong infusion of chamomile, marigold, comfrey or marshmallow
Essential oil of your choice

Place the herb in a pan and cover with water, the herb, if fresh, having first been bruised. Bring to the boil and then simmer for 10 minutes, no steam being allowed to escape. Leave to infuse for 6 hours and put in a heat-proof glass bowl with the soap that has been grated. Place this over a pan of simmering water and stir until the soap has melted and blended with the infusion. Leave to cool slightly then add an essential oil to improve the fragrance. Grease or oil the shell and heart moulds (bun or jelly moulds or plastic sandpit shapes can be used) and pour in the mixture. Leave to set for several days. When firm remove from the moulds and turn once a week until the soap has hardened, to allow even drying out. Wipe away any traces of oil or grease from the soaps and wrap them in coloured tissue paper.

Elderflowers are a renowned beauty aid. They will cleanse, moisturize and lighten the complexion and, fortunately, flower abundantly in

Fruit of elderberry tree

Herbal cosmetic preparations: soap, elderflower cream and lavender vinegar.

the wild. This cream will help keep the complexion clear and smooth away lines.

Elderflower cream
½pt (280ml/1¼cups) of freshly picked elder-flowers
6 fl oz (170ml/¾cup) of sweet almond oil
1tbs of anhydrous lanolin
1-3 drops of an essential oil such as lemon or lavender. Optional.

Place the lanolin in a bowl set over a pan of simmering water and melt, then beat in the almond oil. Remove the elderflowers from the stalks and add to the oil and lanolin and simmer for half an hour. Then strain and allow the cream to cool slightly before putting it in screw-top jars.

Add a drop or two of an essential oil to improve the scent of the cream if you wish.

The old-fashioned scent of lavender is always a delight and it is also beneficial to the skin, the herb being an antiseptic and stimulant. Our skin is covered with a thin layer of acid that protects it from infection but this can be removed by using an alkaline rather than acid vegetable oil soap or cosmetic. Rinsing the already cleansed face with lavender vinegar mixed half and half with water, will restore the balance.

Lavender vinegar
2 handfuls of fresh or dried lavender flowers
1oz (28g/2tbs) of powdered orris root
1pt (600ml/2½cups) of cider vinegar

Place all the ingredients in a screw-top jar and leave to steep for 4 weeks. Then strain and bottle.

Herbs and Cooking

The use of fresh and dried herbs in cookery is now quite widespread. The lady of the house might no longer have a still room in which to concoct special brews and sweetmeats but her kitchen shelves invariably boast a collection of herbs, and one or two different oils, vinegars or conserves. Here are some variations on some of the herbs, oils, vinegars and conserves that can be stored and used at will to enhance the flavour of a dish or add that extra dash of interest.

Herb vinegars are superb for adding a piquancy to a sauce, relish or stew, salad dressing or marinade. They are easy to make and keep well.

Herb vinegar
Pour 1pt (600ml/2½cups) of cider or white wine vinegar over 6tbs of lightly chopped or crushed herbs such as rosemary, French tarragon, thyme, marjoram, basil, sage or mint. Mustard seeds, chillis and peppercorns can be added according to taste. Cover and leave to steep for a few weeks, then strain. Boil the vinegar and then bottle, adding a fresh sprig of the herb used before sealing with a non-metallic stopper.

A marinade can make an otherwise flavourless or cheap cut of meat something special and can also help to tenderize it. There are mint marinades for lamb, rosemary for chicken or the following recipe which is suitable for fish. Wine or wine vinegar should take the place of lemon juice when marinating meat.

Fennel marinade
4tbs (56ml/¼cup) of olive oil
Juice of 1 large lemon plus grated rind
1 chopped shallot or small onion
2 cloves of garlic crushed
1tbs of chopped parsley
1tbs of chopped fennel
Salt and pepper

Mix the ingredients together and pour over the fish and leave in the cool for several hours to allow the marinade to seep in. Baste with the marinade during the cooking process.

Neat pats of herb butter melting on a portion of grilled meat or fish look as good as they taste and are easily made in quantity and stored in the freezer until needed. They can also be served with hot rolls or French bread. Various herbs can be used and the proportions should be as follows: to every 8oz (250g/2½cups) of butter add 4tbs (heaped) of the chopped herb, salt and pepper, the juice of a lemon or 3 large cloves of garlic. Garlic goes best with red meat and the herbs rosemary, sage, chervil and marjoram, while the butter containing the grated rind and juice of a lemon goes best with fish, vegetables and white meat and the herbs tarragon, parsley, fennel or lemon thyme.

A bouquet garni is a bunch of fresh sprigs of mixed herbs or a small sachet containing dried herbs. The latter is easier to use in soups and stews as it does not break up and can be removed with ease when the cooking process is over. The traditional ingredients are 2 sprigs of parsley, 1 bay leaf and 1 sprig of tarragon. Other herbs such as garlic, celery or fennel can be added, depending on whether the dish is meat- or fish-based.

Fines herbes are a mix of the dried or fresh leaves only of 2 parts parsley, 1 of chives and chervil and ½ of tarragon. Always acceptable presents to any keen cook, the little muslin sachets or bags of bouquet garni or *fines herbes* can be wrapped in attractive green- or red-checked cotton and tied with coloured thread.

The following herb jelly is an excellent accompaniment to hot or cold ham, chicken, duck, pork or lamb.

Herb jelly
Apples
Water
Malt vinegar
Fresh herb
Sugar

Coursely cut up the apples without peeling or coring them and discard any rotten bits. Place in

Culinary herbs, vinegars, jellies, bouquet garni, *fines herbes*, herbal butters and marinades.

a pan and cover with water and vinegar: use ¼pt (140ml/½cup) of vinegar to every 1pt (600ml/ 2½cups) of water. Add a good handful of sprigs of one herb, either parsley, thyme, sage or mint, and simmer with the apples until they have been reduced to a pulp. Ladle the contents of the pan into a jelly bag and strain. Measure the strained juice into a preserving pan and to every 1pt (600ml/2½cups) of liquid add 1lb (450g) of preserving or granulated sugar. Dissolve the sugar in the liquid over a low heat, then bring to the boil and cook until setting point has been reached. Skim any froth from the surface, allow to cool for a few minutes, and to every 1lb (450g) of apples used stir in 1tbs of the chopped herb. Pour into warmed jam jars and cover.

THREE VARIATIONS ON A HERBAL THEME

CULINARY CHEQUER-BOARD HERB GARDEN

A certain amount of fresh herbs will be grown in a kitchen garden, either as companion plants, or for culinary and other purposes. But the convenience to the cook of having herbs close to hand, of not having to change footwear and possibly tramp a distance to gather them in bad weather, is always appreciated.

They can be grown in window-boxes, strawberry and other pots and troughs or planted in between paving stones, creating a chequer-board effect. This design adapts equally well to a small paved garden where space is limited, or to a large plot. The stones or bricks create a series of tiny gardens, one for each herb, that are easy to tend and also effective in preventing an invasive plant from spreading too far. Mint should always be treated with caution and be planted in a bottomless bucket or pot, or have its roots surrounded with slates lowered at least 1ft (30cm) down into the ground.

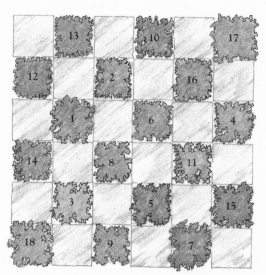

The chequer-board garden can be incorporated into a terrace around the house where it will stand as an attractive feature in itself. Or set into the lawn, with creeping lawn herbs that release their scent when trodden on, planted on its outer edges. The following list is a good mix of annual, biennial and perennial culinary herbs. Different varieties of, for example, mint or thyme can be added or amended according to individual taste.

SUGGESTED HERBS FOR THE CULINARY CHEQUER-BOARD GARDEN
(a = annual; b = bulb; p = perennial;
sh = shrub; h = hardy; hp = hardy perennial)

1 Borage a, *Borago officinalis*
2 Caraway b, *Carum carvi*
3 Chervil a, *Anthriscus cerefolium*
4 Chives or Garlic chives p, *Allium schoenoprasum*
5 Dill a, *Anethum graveolens*
6 Fennel p, *Foeniculum vulgare*
7 Garlic b, *Allium sativum*
8 Lovage p, *Levisticum officinale*
9 Mint p, *Mentha species*
10 Parsley b, *Petroselinum crispum*
11 Rosemary p, *Rosmarinus officinalis*
12 Sage p, *Salvia officinalis*
13 Sorrel h, *Rumex acetosa*
14 French tarragon hp, *Artemisia dracunculus*
15 Thyme p, *Thymus vulgaris*
16 Winter savory hp, *Satureja montana*
17 Creeping chamomile p, *Chamaemelum nobile* 'Treneague'
18 Creeping thyme p, *Thymus serpyllum*

FRAGRANT HERB KNOT GARDEN

A knot was an important ingredient of the well-dressed Tudor garden and was frequently laid out to resemble the pattern of an ornate plaster or

carved wooden ceiling, a family emblem or the entwined initials of its owners. It would be placed beneath the windows of the house in order that its intricate pattern could be fully admired from an upstairs window; it was a practical as well as a decorative feature. When the hedges were cut, the clippings were used for strewing or in the still room, and the knot itself often masked from view by the linen that was spread over it to dry. While drying, the linen would absorb the fragrance of the herbs. The design of what was known as the closed knot was an intricate pattern of neatly clipped hedges interspersed with gravel. The open knot is less complex and leaves more room to plant low-growing, flowering and other subjects in between the pattern of hedges.

A formal and disciplined feature, it is essential that the knot's clean-cut lines are preserved. The herbs used must not be allowed to 'wander' or seed themselves freely. If possible the colours and

Below
A formal knot garden composed of dwarf box, cotton lavender, winter savory and wall germander.

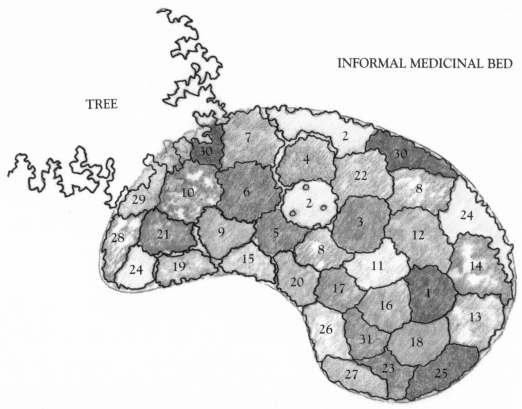

INFORMAL MEDICINAL BED

TREE

texture of the low hedges must vary to add interest and the plants should have a neat habit. The hedging material is best grown from cuttings a year before the knot is laid out, though dwarf box will take considerably longer to mature and should be grown well in advance of the others. Having prepared the soil, carefully peg out the pattern before planting and lay gravel in the gaps between the hedges. This will cut down on weeding and also highlight the design.

SUGGESTED HERBS FOR THE FRAGRANT KNOT GARDEN
(p = perennial)

1 Dwarf box p, *Buxus sempervirens* 'Suffruticosa'
2 Cotton lavender p, *Santolina chamaecyparissus* nana
3 Hyssop p, *Hyssopus officinalis*
4 Bergamot p, *Monarda didyma*
5 Sage p, *Salvia officinalis*, 'Purpurascens', 'Icterina' or 'Tricolor'

6 Variegated lemon balm p, *Melissa officinalis* 'Aurea'
7 Curry plant p, *Helichrysum angustifolium*
8 Standard honeysuckle p, *Lonicera periclymenum*
9 Lemon thyme p, *Thymus citriodorus* 'Aureus'
10 Golden marjoram p, *Origanum vulgare* 'Aureum'
11 Lavender p, *Lavandula angustifolia* 'Hidcote'
12 White violas p, *Viola cornuta* 'Alba'
13 Old-fashioned pink p, *Dianthus* 'Mrs Sinkins'

INFORMAL BED OF MEDICINAL HERBS
The range of medicinal herbs is considerable but a certain number are too dangerous to use in home made remedies – foxgloves, hellebores and hemlock being examples. Others are no longer considered beneficial, are poisonous or thought of as weeds by the unitiated; but all have either a historical significance or aesthetic reason to be included in a medicinal herb garden.

This informal bed will incorporate herbs such as those mentioned along with varieties that, used correctly and with care, can cause no harm and hopefully are beneficial to those that grow them. If there is any doubt as to the best way to use a medicinal herb, seek professional advice. Also do not allow those who are unfamiliar with the plants to pick and savour them at random as they might do with culinary herbs. Certain medicinal plants should only be used externally. The foliage of others has an adverse effect on the system while the root or seeds has a beneficial effect, or vice versa.

The advantages of growing herbs, or any group of plants, in an island bed are many. The contents can be admired from all angles and the bed can accommodate a pleasing mix of shrubs, perennials and annuals. Tall plants placed at the centre of the bed are supported by those that surround them. (The only plant in the plan below that will need staking is the golden hop. A focal point of the bed, this is best trained up a pyramid of stakes.) Some of the herbs need a degree of shade or like moist conditions, the western end of the bed provides these.

A group of small plants is always a more attractive sight than randomly placed single specimens, hence the space allowed on the plan for several marigolds, heartease pansies, thyme and feverfew. If you intend to ignore the purist attitude when stocking the bed and the plants are not going to be used for home remedies, extra interest can be added by using different varieties

of several herbs: white foxgloves, unusual hellebores, silver and lemon thyme, bronze fennel and variegated lemon balm and rue, can replace the common, strictly medicinal varieties.

SUGGESTED HERBS FOR THE INFORMAL MEDICINAL BED
(b=biennial; p=perennial; a=annual; sh=shrub)

1 Rosemary sh, *Rosmarinus officinalis*
2 Golden hop p, *Humulus lupulus* 'Aureus'
3 Evening primrose b, *Oenothera biennis*
4 Fennel p, *Foeniculum vulgare*
5 Tansy p, *Tanacetum vulgare*
6 Angelica b & p, *Angelica archangelica*
7 Elecampane p, *Inula helenium*
8 Foxglove p, *Digitalis purpurea*
9 Meadowsweet p, *Filipendula ulmaria*
10 Marshmallow p, *Althaea officinalis*
11 Apothecary's rose sh, *Rosa gallica* var *officinalis*
12 Clary sage b, *Salvia sclarea* var *turkestanica*
13 English lavender p, *Lavandula spica*
14 Yarrow p, *Achillea millefolium*
15 Lemon balm p, *Melissa officinalis*
16 Southernwood p, *Artemisia abrotanum*
17 Rue p, *Ruta graveolens*
18 Sage sh, *Salvia officinalis*
19 Marigold a, *Calendula officinalis*
20 Feverfew p, *Tanacetum parthenium* 'Aureum', formerly *Chrysanthemum*
21 Blue flag iris, *Iris versicolor*
22 Golden sage sh, *Salvia officinalis* 'Icterina'
23 Golden marjoram p, *Origanum vulgare* 'Aureum'
24 Lady's mantle p, *Alchemilla mollis*
25 German chamomile p, *Matricaria recutita*
26 Heartsease a, *Viola tricolor*
27 Thyme p, *Thymus vulgaris*, *Thymus x citriodorus* 'Silver Queen'
28 Lily of the valley p, *Convallaria majalis*
29 Hellebore p, *Helleborus orientalis*
30 Lungwort p, *Pulmonaria officinalis*
31 Garlic p, *Allium sativum*

Eyebright

PUTTING THEORY
INTO PRACTICE

HEDGED ORNAMENTAL
HERB GARDEN ON DARTMOOR

Attached to a small nursery, situated in the spectacular countryside of Dartmoor National Park, this herb garden was started in 1983 by Hugh and Sally Wetherbee. The aim was to create a colourful display for the visitors to the nursery, show the growing habit of various herbs and also to offer visitors inspiration and ideas for incorporating herbs into their own gardens, however large or small. The design, content and size are particularly easy to relate to varied situations. Informative as well as attractive, it demonstrates how herbs can be used to decorate a garden at the same time as offering many practical uses.

Created on a long, narrow strip of land that faces north-east and slopes down to a lane, the herb garden stands parallel to the lane in the most sheltered part of the garden. The soil is slightly acid and free-draining. The beech hedge, placed two deep and 18in (45cm) apart, was not only planted to provide extra protection but also to give the garden a private, secret, character. It is still young, as the illustrations show, and can only enhance the overall picture as it matures. The arbour constructed of timber is a welcome accent of vertical interest, being entwined with climbing roses that add a brilliant dash of colour as well as fragrance. A grass path measuring 3ft 6in (1m) wide runs down the centre of the garden, the small statue at the far end acting as a

Opposite and above
Catmint, bergamot and marigolds are among the herbs which enrich this hedged herb garden with rustic arbour.

focal point. Standing beyond this at the end of the garden is a bed set above a low, dry-stone wall and area of gravel. This is planted with small creeping herbs such as pennyroyal and chamomile, and is easy to view being set slightly higher than the rest of the garden. In the long beds either side of the grass path are herbs mixed with some herbaceous perennials, which demonstates how well they adapt to and blend with cultivated, ornamental plants.

A tub made from a half barrel stands near the house suitably planted with low-growing and shallow-rooted herbs such as creeping thymes and the alpine strawberry. Always a useful and decorative feature in a garden, tubs have the extra advantage of being easily covered over in mid-winter when tender plants might otherwise be damaged by a severe frost. The top 2in (5cm)

of the compost are renewed annually, and the tub watered regularly during the growing season.

Sally Wetherbee uses her herbs extensively in the kitchen, freezing many for use in winter and preserving others such as tarragon in vinegar. A favourite recipe is one for *fines herbes* vinaigrette:

1 tsp chopped chives
1 tsp chopped parsley
1 tsp dried mustard
1 tsp curry powder
1 tsp salt
Large pinch freshly ground pepper
1 crushed garlic clove
2 tsp brown sugar
6 fl oz (170ml/¾cup) olive oil
4tbs (56ml/¼cup) tarragon vinegar
2 tsp lemon juice

Place all the ingredients in a screw-top jar and shake vigorously. Use as required, storing the surplus in the fridge.

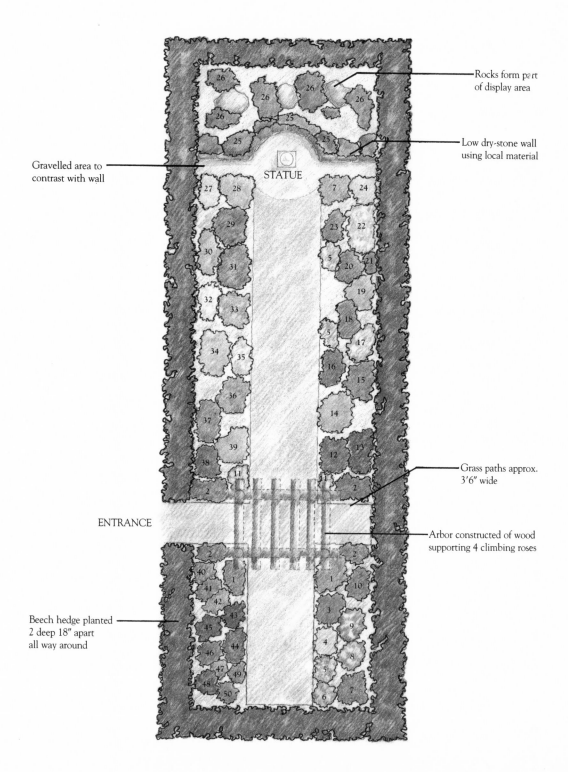

Rocks form part
of display area

Low dry-stone wall
using local material

Gravelled area to
contrast with wall

STATUE

Grass paths approx.
3'6" wide

ENTRANCE

Arbor constructed of wood
supporting 4 climbing roses

Beech hedge planted
2 deep 18" apart
all way around

PLANTS GROWN IN THE HEDGED ORNAMENTAL HERB GARDEN AT DEVON HERBS

(a = annual; b = biennial; p = perennial; hp = hardy perennial)

1 Catmint p, *Nepeta mussini*
2 Hyssop p, *Hyssopus officinalis*
3 German chamomile a, *Matricaria recutita*
4 *Sedum album* p
5 Heartsease a, *Viola tricolor*
6 Pot marigold a, *Calendula officinalis*
7 Wormwood p, *Artemisia absinthium*
8 Evening primrose b, *Oenothera biennis*
9 Bergamot hp, *Monarda didyma*
10 Hyssop p, *Hyssopus officinalis*
11 Cowslip p, *Primula veris*
12 Pot marjoram p, *Origanum onites*
13 Comfrey p, *Symphytum officinale*
14 Purple sage p, *Salvia officinalis* 'Purpurascens'
15 Sage p, *Salvia officinalis*
16 Roman chamomile p, *Chamaemelum nobile*
17 Lupins (various colours and varieties) p, *Lupinus species*
18 Curry plant p, *Helichrysum angustifolium*
19 Blazing star p, *Liatris spicata*
20 Rosemary, *Rosmarinus officinalis* 'Miss Jessopp's Upright'
21 Curled-leafed tansy p, *Tanacetum densum*
22 Michaelmas daisy p, *Aster x frikartii*
23 Salad burnet p, *Poterium sanguisorba*
24 Angelica b, *Angelica archangelica*
25 Variety of creeping plants grown over low stone wall:
Pennyroyal p, *Mentha pulegium*
Lawn chamomile p, *Chamaemelum nobile* 'Treneague'
Creeping thymes p: caraway thyme, *T. herba barona*; *T. serpyllum*; Doone Valley
26 Variety of upright thymes p:
Common thyme, *T. vulgaris*
Lemon thyme, *T. citriodorus*
Golden lemon thyme, *T. vulgaris citriodorus* 'Aureus'
Porlock thyme, *Thymus* 'Porlock'

27 Lovage p, *Levisticum officinale*
28 Variegated grass p, *Alopecurus pratensis* 'Aureo-variegatus'
29 Old English lavender p, *Lavendula spica*
30 Dyer's chamomile p, *Anthemis tinctoria*
31 Cotton lavender p, *Santolina chamaecyparissus*
32 Lupins p, *Lupinus*
33 Lavender p, *Lavendula angustifolia* 'Hidcote'
34 Variegated lemon golden balm p, *Melissa officinalis* 'Aurea'
35 Double-flowered Roman chamomile p, *Chamaelum nobile*
36 Sweet cicely hp, *Myrrhis odorata*
37 Bronze fennel p, *Foeniculum purpureum*
38 Fennel p, *Foeniculum vulgare*
39 Woad b, *Isatis tinctoria*
40 Juniper p, *Juniperis communis* (male)
41 Juniper p, *Juniperis communis* (female)
42 Rosemary p, *Rosmarinus officinalis*
43 French tarragon p, *Artemisia dracunculus*
44 Curled parsley b, *Petroselinum crispum*
45 French/Italian parsley b, *Petroselinum neapolitanum*
46 Sage p, *Salvia officinalis*
47 Borage a, *Borago officinalis*
48 Lovage p, *Levisticum officinalis*
49 Winter savory p, *Satureja montana*
50 Alpine strawberry p, *Fragaria alpina* 'Alexandria'

INFORMAL MEDICINAL AND FRAGRANT HERB GARDEN AT POLYPHANT

The medicinal and fragrant herb garden at Polyphant, near Launceston in Cornwall, is laid out in what was once an old cider orchard that stood near the early seventeenth-century house. Some of the old apple trees still shade the lawns and beds of this subtle and charming garden that was begun by Jane Deighton in the late 1970s.

Beside the garden that measures 80ft (24m) by 60ft (18m) is a rebuilt stone barn that once housed the cider press. Golden hop and honeysuckle now scramble up its south-facing wall. Jane, who has always been an enthusiastic

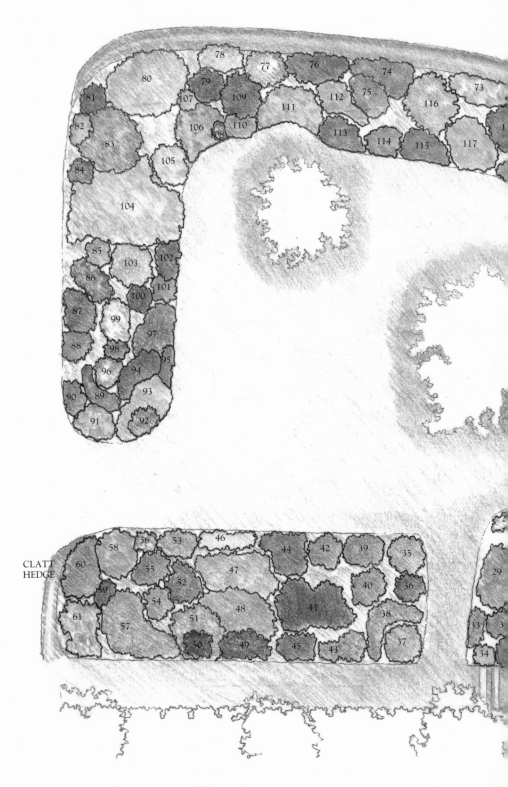

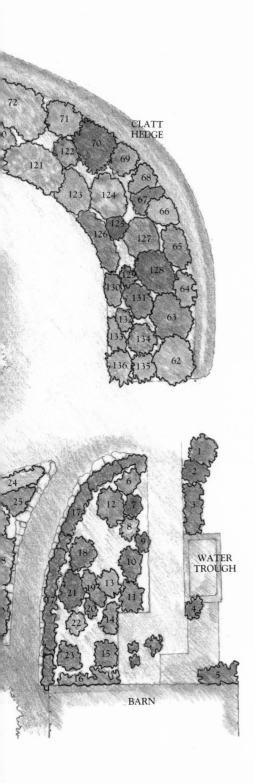

gardener, when planning the garden decided that it should have a definite theme. Although it would contain her ever-increasing collection of medicinal, culinary and fragrant herbs and consequently have many practical uses, its appearance would have to satisfy her ideal combination of colour and form. Maximum use has been made of the characteristic gentle colours and varied foliage shape, size and textures of the diverse collection of herbs.

The plants are imaginatively placed to flatter or emphasize their neighbour's individual qualities; the overall effect is of a harmonious and well-balanced picture. There are many lessons to be learnt from Polyphant that can be applied to the ornamental as well as the herb garden.

Set on slightly acid, free-draining soil, the garden stands on blue elvin, a stone that is quarried locally. An interesting and attractive feature of its design is the bank of turf that partially surrounds it. Locally this is known as a clatt hedge and is traditional to regions of Cornwall and Devon where stone for wall-making is not immediately available. A typical hedge is usually 6ft (1.8m) high and 6ft (1.8m) wide at the base. Though smaller in scale, the one at Polyphant serves as a useful boundary. The plants directly in front of it include elecampane, lovage and mulleins, all of which grow tall in the summer giving an enclosed feeling to this part of the garden.

Most aromatic herbs are good companion plants, though care has been taken to place those that are less neighbourly – such as rue, fennel and wormwood – where they will not interfere with the growth of the others. Being an organic garden no artificial or chemical fertilizers or pesticides are used. It is especially important that plants used for medicine and food should be grown naturally. The borders are given a top dressing of home-made compost every year and comfrey is used as a green manure.

Full use is made of the herbs that grow in the garden. Salad herbs such as fennel, salad burnet

The bold foliage and golden flowers of elecampane in the clatt-hedge border at Polyphant.

and French sorrel are grown in and among increasingly better-known medicinal herbs such as white horehound, feverfew and pasque flower. Many, such as chamomile and lemon balm are used for tisanes, both pleasurable as well as remedial. Some plants are of mainly historical interest and there are several collections of certain genera such as *Digitalis*, *Symphytum*, *Thymus* and *Aconitum*.

PLANTS GROWN IN THE INFORMAL MEDICINAL AND FRAGRANT HERB GARDEN AT POLYPHANT
(a = annual; b = biennial; p = perennial)

Small beds beside the barn

1 Tree lupin p, *Lupinus arboreus*
2 Variegated box sh, *Buxus variegata*
3 Roman chamomile p, *Chamaemelum nobile*
4 Thyme p, *Thymus species*
5 Variegated ground ivy p, *Glechoma hederacea variegata*
6 Golden sage p, *Salvia officinalis* 'Icterina'
7 English mace p, *Achillea declorans*
8 Rose p, *Rosa gallica* 'Tuscany'
9 Thyme p, *Thymus vulgaris*
10 Lavender p, *Lavandula* 'Loddon Pink'
11 *Artemisia triloba* p
12 Anise hyssop p, (various including *Agastache anethiodora*)
13 Motherwort p, *Leonurus cardiaca*
14 Wall germander p, *Teucriuim chamaedrys*
15 Rosemary p, *Rosmarinus officinalis* (broad-leaf form)
16 Golden hop p, *Humulus lupulus* 'Aureus'
17 Thymes p, (various including *T.micans*, *T.herba-barona*, *T.cocineus*, *T.albus* 'Annie Hall'
18 Rue p, *Ruta graveolens*
19 A form of sea holly p, *Eryngium planum*
20 Tree onion p, *Allium cepa proliferum*
21 Curry plant p, *Helichrysum angustifolium*

22 Pink-flowered chives p, *Allium schoenoprasum roseum*

23 Saw wort p, *Serratula tinctoria*

24 Bugle p, *Adjuga reptans variegata*

25 Porlock thyme p, *Thymus* 'Porlock'

26 Cheddar pink p, *Dianthus gratianopolitanus*

27 Soapwort p, *Saponaria officinalis*

28 Pink flowered chives p, *Allium schoenoprasum roseum*

29 A form of wormwood p, *Artemisia absinthium* 'Powys Castle'

30 Pink-flowered hyssop p, *Hyssopus officinalis rosea*

31 Gold-tipped marjoram p, *Origanum vulgare variegatum*

32 Rosemary p, *Rosmarinus officinalis*

33 Curled tansy p, *Tanacetum densum*

34 White-flowered betony p, *Stachys officinalis albus* (old name *Betonica*)

Flowers in the north border

35 Cotton lavender p, *Santolina chamaecyparissus*

36 Lavender p, *Lavandula* 'Loddon Pink'

37 Monkshood p, *Aconitum anglicum, A. bicolor, A. vulparia* and *A. carneum*

38 Ginger mint p, *Mentha gentilis* 'Variegata'

39 Lavender p, *Lavandula* 'Munstead dwarf'

40 Green-leaved cotton lavender p, *Santolina virens*

41 Silver-leafed sage p, *Salvia officinalis*

42 Golden sage p, *Salvia officinalis* 'Icterina'

43 Winter aconites b, *Eranthus hyemalis*

44 Thyme p, *Thymus vulgaris*

45 Purple sage p, *Salvia officinalis* 'Purpurascens'

46 Self heal p, *Prunella x webbiana* 'Loveliness'

47 Geranium p, *Geranium macrorrhizum*

48 Golden marjoram p, *Origanum vulgare* 'Aureum'

49 Lovage p, *Levisticum officinale*

50 Purple sage p, *Salvia officinalis* 'Purpurascens'

51 Evening primrose p, *Oenothera biennis*

52 Wild marjoram p, *Origanum vulgare*

53 Cheddar pink p, *Dianthus gratianopolitanus*

54 Cotton lavender p, *Santolina chamaecyparissus*

55 Porlock thyme p, *Thymus* 'Porlock'

56 Dwarf lady's mantle p, *Alchemilla conjuncta*

57 Bowles mint p, *mentha rotundifolia*

58 Golden sage p, *Salvia officinale* 'Icterina'

59 Great burnet p, *Sanguisorba officinalis*

60 Apple mint p, *Mentha suaveolens*

61 Sweetbriar rose p, *Rosa rubiginosa*

Herbs in the south border

62 Golden sage p, *Salvia officinalis* 'Icterina'

63 Wild majoram p, *Origanum vulgare*

64 Purple coneflower p, *Echinacea purpurea*

65 Poke root p, *Phytolacca americana*

66 Fennel p, *Feoniculum vulgare*

67 Mullein p, *Verbascum thapsus*

68 Chicory b, *Cichorium intybus*

69 Mugwort p, *Artemisia vulgaris*

70 Curled mint p, *Mentha spicata crispa*

71 Peppermint p, *Mentha piperita*

72 Lovage p, *Levisticum officinale*

73 White muskmallow p, *Althaea moschata* 'Alba'

74 Variegated lemon balm p, *Melissa officinalis variegata*

75 Sweet rocket p, *Hesperis matronalis*

76 Hemp agrimony p, *Eupatorium purpureum*

77 Teazle b, *Dipsacus fullonum*

78 Bugbane p, *Cimicifuga racemosa*

79 Dyer's greenweed p, *Genista tinctoria*

80 Elecampane p, *Inula helenium*

81 Purple sage p, *Salvia officinalis* 'Purpurascens'

82 Alaskan yarrow p, *Achillea borealis*

83 Sweet cicely p, *Myrrhis odorata*

84 Monkshood b, *Aconitum anglicum*

85 Cotton lavender p, *Santolina virens*

86 Monkshood p, *Aconitum anglicum*

87 White rosemary p, *Rosmarinus officinalis albus*

88 Wormwood p, *Artemisia absinthium* 'Lambrook Silver'

89 Sweet rocket p, *Hesperis matronalis*

90 Sage p, *Salvia officinalis*
91 Evening primrose p, *Oenothera biennis*
92 Cotton lavender p, *Santolina chamaecyparissus*
93 Jacob's ladder p, *Polemonium caeruleum*
94 Scullcap p, *Scutellaria lateriflora*
95 Caraway thyme p, *Thymus herba-barona*
96 Marshmallow p, *Althaea officinalis*
97 Cultivated form of wormwood p, *Artemisia absinthium* 'Powys Castle'
98 Fennel p, *Feoniculum vulgare*
99 White muskmallow, *Althaea moschata* 'Alba'
100 Camphor plant p, *Balsamita tomentosum*
101 Lavender p, *Lavandula angustifolia* 'Hidcote' (dark blue form)
102 Sweet woodruff p, *Asperula odorata*
103 Jupiter's distaff p, *Salvia glutinosa*
104 Double soapwort p, *Saponaria officinalis* 'Flora Plena'
105 Lady's mantle p, *Alchemilla mollis*
106 Cowslip p, *Primula veris*
107 Variegated wall germander p, *Teucrium chamaedrys* 'Variegatum'
108 Double meadowsweet p, *Filipendula hexapetala* 'Flore Pleno'
109 Rosemary p, *Rosmarinus officinalis*
110 Lavender p, *Lavandula officinalis*
111 Cowslip p, *Primula veris*
112 Jacob's ladder p, *Polemonium caeruleum*
113 Southernwood p, *Artemisia abrotanum*
114 Silver variegated thyme p, *Thymus* 'Silver Posy'
115 Curled marjoram p, *Origanum aureum crispum*
116 Silver leafed sage p, *Salvia officinalis*
117 Variegated lemon balm p, *Melissa officinalis* 'Aureum'
118 Rosemary p, *Rosmarinus* 'Miss Jessopp's upright'
119 Lavender p, *Lavandula angustifolia* 'Munstead Dwarf'
120 Large yellow foxglove p, *Digitalis grandiflora*
121 Soapwort p, *Saponaria officinalis*
122 Purple coneflower p, *Echinacea purpurea*

123 Silver-leafed sage p, *Salvia officinalis*
124 Lady's mantle p, *Alchemilla mollis*
125 Chives p, *Allium schoenoprasum*
126 Creeping thymes p, (various)
127 Purple sage p, *Salvia officinalis* 'Purpurascens'
128 Great burnet p, *Sanguisorba officinalis*
129 Iris p, *Iris pallida*
130 Caraway thyme p, *Thymus herba-barona*
131 Curry plant p, *Helichrysum angustifolium*
132 Cotton lavender p, *Santolina chamaecyparissus*
133 Curled marjoram p, *Origanum aureum crispum*
134 Monkshood p, *Aconitum anglicum*
135 Jacob's ladder p, *Polemonium caeruleum*
136 Yellow foxglove p, *Digitalis lutea*

A FORMAL SUNKEN HERB GARDEN AT HATFIELD HOUSE

Elizabeth I spent much of her childhood at Hatfield, and it was here that she learnt of her accession to the throne in 1558. The present building is one of England's most splendid period houses, and is surrounded by a suitably magnificent garden.

It has been the home of the Cecil family since the early seventeenth century when James I and Robert Cecil, Lord Salisbury, exchanged estates: Hatfield fell into their hands, and James acquired the Cecil's old home, Theobalds. Built by Lord Burghley, Salisbury's father and Elizabeth's chief minister, Theobalds no longer exists, but was famed for its gardens which were in the charge of the aforementioned herbalist, John Gerard. Gerard gained much from working for Lord Burghley and showed his gratitude and respect by dedicating his 'Herball' to him. But it was Lord Salisbury who was to transform the new estate, Hatfield, by rebuilding the old episcopal palace in fine contemporary style and laying out elaborate new gardens.

These boasted complex waterworks; a flourishing vineyard; a stream decorated with shells, serpents, fish, and leaves made of lead; and an impressive collection of newly introduced plants, trees and shrubs.

Many of these rarities were collected by Lord Salisbury's gardeners the John Tradescants, father and son, whose names are inextricably entwined with that of the gardens at Hatfield. They could be called England's first plant-hunters, and introduced to this country the now familiar Virginia creeper, Michaelmas daisy, lilac, acacia, and occidental plane. The latter was crossed with the oriental variety and produced the now familiar London plane.

The gardens have seen many changes over the centuries, their design conforming to the fashion of the day. During the eighteenth century the Jacobean gardens were swept away and replaced by a then fashionable landscape that ran up to the very walls of the house, but they have gradually been restored to their original style since early this century. The present Marchioness of Salisbury is to be thanked for much that can be seen today – the period design, content and atmosphere of the gardens that blend so harmoniously with the architecture of the Jacobean house built of warm red brick.

The herb garden that lies on the terraces to the west of the house, is sunken and set around a sundial. Measuring approximately 24×14 yds (22×13m), it is approached at either end by a flight of steps from the tops of which its full extent can be admired. Strictly formal in design and divided into four parts by gravel and paved paths, its planting is, by contrast, delightfully informal, wonderfully scented and of subtle colouring.

Gardening methods are strictly organic at Hatfield, where the soil lies on free-draining gravel and is just on the acid side of neutral. A three-year mulching programme is carried out: in the first year the garden is mulched with farmyard manure, in the second with garden compost, and in the third it is given a feed of calcified seaweed. Sprays and artificial fertilizers are never used. Herbs of all kinds have been grown here, early

varieties and an exuberance of old-fashioned roses being much in evidence.

PLANTS GROWN IN THE FORMAL SUNKEN HERB GARDEN AT HATFIELD HOUSE

(a = annual; b = biennial; p = perennial; s = shrub; t = tree)
Section 1

A Small crescent bed nearest the sundial

1 Chervil a, *Anthriscus cerefolium*
2 Thyme p, *Thymus*
3 Standard woodbine honeysuckle s, *Lonicera periclymenum*
4 Standard woodbine honeysuckle s, *Lonicera periclymenum*
5 Spearmint p, *Mentha spicata*
6 Marigold a, *Calendula officinalis*
7 Pot marjoram p, *Origanum onites*

B Middle crescent bed

1 Curled-leafed tansy p, *Tanacetum densum*
2 Onion b, *Allium moly*
3 Tulip b, *Tulipa marjoletii*
4 Provins rose s, *Rosa gallica* 'Belle Isis'
5 Tulip b, *Tulipa clusiana*
6 Salad burnet p, *Poterium sanguisorba*
7 Chervil a, *Anthriscus cerefolium*
8 Provins rose s, *Rose gallica* 'Versicolor' syn. 'Rosa Mundi'
9 Lavender p, *Lavandula spica* 'Loddon Pink'
10 Damask rose s, *Rosa damascena* 'Leda'
11 Pineapple mint p, *Mentha sauveolens* 'Variegata'
12 Provins rose s, *Rosa gallica* 'Empress Josephine'
13 Moss rose s, *Rosa muscosa* 'Soupert et Nothing'
14 Welsh onion b, *Allium fistulosum*

C Large corner bed

1 Sweetbriar rose s, *Rosa rubiginosa* 'Amy Robsart'

2 Tulip b, *Tulipa* 'Rembrandt'
3 Tulip b, *Tulipa* 'Rembrandt'
4 Angelica p, *Angelica archangelica*
5 Tansy p, *Tanacetum vulgare*
6 Standard woodbine honeysuckle p, *Lonicera periclymenum*
7 Rosemary p, *Rosmarinus officinalis*
8 Woad a, *Isatis tinctoria*
9 Damask rose s, *Rosa damascena* 'Celsiana'
10 Rue p, *Ruta graveolens*
11 Catmint a, *Calamintha grandiflora*
12 Fennel p, *Foeniculum vulgare*
13 Rose s, *Rosa* 'Soupert et Nothing'
14 Grecian sage p, *Salvia heamatodes*
15 Apothecary's rose s, *Rosa gallica officinalis*
16 Miniature curry plant p, *Helichrysum italicum*
17 Foxglove b, *Digitalis*
18 Provins rose s, *Rosa gallica* 'Tuscany Superb'
19 Purple sage p, *Salvia officinalis* 'Purpurascens'
20 Hybrid perpetual rose s, *Rosa* 'Baronne Prévost'
21 Tulip b, *Tulipa marjoletii*
22 Nasturtium a, *Trapaeolum majus*
23 Provins rose s, *Rosa gallica* 'Velutinaeflora'
24 Golden sage p, *Salvia officinalis* 'Icterina'
25 Borage a, *Boraga officinalis*
26 Laced pink p, *Dianthus*
27 Polyanthus p, *Primula* 'Gold Laced'
28 Globe artichoke p, *Cynara scolymus*
29 Tree onion b, *Allium cepa proliferum*
30 Rose s, *Rosa*
31 Mint p, *Mentha*
32 Fragrant thyme p, *Thymus fragrantissimus*
33 Cotton lavender p, *Santolina chamaecyparissus*
34 English mace p, *Achillea decolorans*
35 Laced pink p, *Dianthus*
36 Lemon balm p, *Melissa officinalis*
37 Tulip b, *Tulipa* 'Rembrandt'
38 Standard woodbine honeysuckle p, *Lonicera periclymenum*
39 Rosemary p, *Rosmarinus officinalis*
40 Sweetbriar rose s, *Rosa rubiginosa* 'Meg Merrilees'

Central sundial and standard honeysuckles, Hatfield.

SECTION 4

SECTION 3

Section 2

A Small crescent bed nearest the sundial

1 Curled-leafed tansy p, *Tanacetum densum*
2 Thyme p, *Thymus*
3 Standard woodbine honeysuckle s, *Lonicera periclymenum*
4 Spearmint p, *Mentha spicata*
5 Standard woodbine honeysuckle s, *Lonicera periclymenum*
6 Pot majoram p, *Origanum onites*

B Middle crescent bed

1 Tulip b, *Tulipa marjoletii*
2 Cabbage rose s, *Rosa centifolia* 'De Meaux'
3 Chicory p, *Cichorium intybus*
4 Cotton lavender p, *Santolina virens*
5 Provins rose s, *Rosa gallica* 'Versicolor' syn. 'Rosa Mundi'
6 Chervil a, *Anthriscus cerefolium*
7 Laced pink p, *Dianthus*
8 Thyme p, *Thymus*
9 Crested cabbage rose s, *Rosa centifolia* 'Chapeau de Napoleon'
10 Iris reticulata b, *Iris reticulata* 'J S Dijt'
11 French tarragon p, *Artemisia dracunculus*
12 Cabbage rose s, *Rosa centifolia* 'Juno'
13 Miniature curry plant p, *Helichrysum italicum*
14 Variegated ginger mint p, *Mentha x gentilis* 'Variegata'

C Large corner bed

1 Sweetbriar rose s, *Rosa rubiginosa* 'Amy Robsart'
2 Standard woodbine honeysuckle p, *Lonicera periclymenum*
3 Applemint p, *Mentha sauveolens*
4 Tansy p, *Tanacetum vulgare*
5 Rosemary p, *Rosmarinus officinalis*
6 Foxglove p, *Digitalis*
7 Tulip b, *Tulipa* 'Rembrandt'
8 Rue p, *Ruta graveolens*
9 Apothecary's rose s, *Rosa gallica officinalis*

10 Damask rose s, *Rosa damascena* 'Celsiana'
11 Common mullein p, *Verbascum thapsiforme*
12 Hyacinth b, *Hyacinthus* 'Salmonetta'
13 Tulip b, *Tulipa marjoletii*
14 Old cabbage rose s, *Rosa centifolia*
15 Globe artichoke p, *Cynara scolymus*
16 Cabbage moss rose s, *Rose centifolia muscosa* 'Marechal Davoust'
17 Cotton lavender p, *Santolina virens*
18 Provins rose s, *Rosa gallica* 'Tuscany Superb'
19 Hyssop p, *Hyssopus officinalis*
20 Southernwood p, *Artemisia abrotanum*
21 Costmary p, *Chrysanthemum balsmita* (formerly *Tanacetum balsamita*)
22 Hybrid tea rose s, *Rosa* 'Los Angeles'
23 Fragrant thyme p, *Thymus odoratissimus*
24 Old cabbage rose s, *Rosa centifolia*
25 Golden sage p, *Salvia officinalis* 'Icterina'
26 Cotton lavender p, *Santolina chamaecyparissus*
27 Provins rose s, *Rosa gallica* 'President de Seze'
28 Tricolour sage p, *Salvia officinalis* 'Tricolor'
29 Polyanthus p, *Primula* 'Gold Laced'
30 Standard woodbine honeysuckle p, *Lonicera periclymenum*
31 Rosemary p, *Rosmarinus officinalis*
32 Sweetbriar rose s, *Rosa rubiginosa* 'Meg Merrilees'

Dog roses

Section 3

A Small crescent bed nearest the sundial

1 Black peppermint p, *Mentha piperita vulgaris*
2 Standard woodbine honeysuckle s, *Lonicera periclymenum*
3 Turkestan tulip b, *Tulipa batalinii* 'Bright Gem'
4 Golden majoram p, *Origanum vulgare* 'Aureum'
5 Pot marigold a, *Calendula officinalis*
6 Wild jonquil b, *Narcissus jonquila* 'Trevithian'
7 Standard woodbine honeysuckle s, *Lonicera periclymenum*
8 *Curled-leafed tansy p, Tanacetum densum*

B Middle crescent bed

1 Borage a, *Borago officinalis*
2 Tulip b, *Tulipa chrysantha*
3 Provins rose s, *Rosa gallica* 'Versicolor' syn. 'Rosa Mundi'
4 Pineapple mint p, *Mentha rotundifolia variegata*
5 Laced pink p, *Dianthus*
6 Lemon balm p, *Melissa officinalis*
7 Thyme p, *Thymus*
8 Laced pink p, *Dianthus*
9 Crested cabbage rose s, *Rosa centifolia* 'Chapeau de Napoleon'
10 Cotton lavender p, *Santolina virens*
11 Tulip b, *Tulipa* 'General de Wet'
12 Sage p, *Salvia multicaulis*
13 Cabbage rose s, *Rosa centifolia* 'De Meaux'
14 Tulip b, *Tulipa clusiana*
15 Wild jonquil b, *Narcissus jonquila*

C Large corner bed

1 Sweetbriar rose s, *Rosa rubiginosa* 'Meg Merrilees
2 Standard woodbine honeysuckle p, *Lonicera periclymenum*
3 Rosemary p, *Rosmarinus officinalis*
4 Cotton lavender p, *Santolina chamaecyparissus*

5 Winter savory p, *Satureja montana*
6 Borage a, *Borago officinalis*
7 Old cabbage rose s, *Rosa centifolia*
8 Jupiter's distaff sage p, *Salvia glutinosa*
9 Tulip b, *Tulipa* 'General de Wet'
10 French tarragon p, *Artemisia drancunculus*
11 Laced pink p, *Dianthus*
12 Common mullein p, *Verbasum thapsiforme*
13 Provins rose s, *Rosa gallica* 'Tuscany Superb'
14 Purple sage p, *Salvia officinalis* 'Purpurascens'
15 Polyanthus p, *Primula* 'Gold Laced'
16 Fennel p, *Foeniculum vulgare*
17 Fragrant thyme p, *Thymus fragrantissimus*
18 Rose s, *Rosa* 'Ma Ponctuée'
19 Alba Rose s, *Rosa alba* 'Maiden's Blush'
20 Hyssop p, *Hyssopus officinalis*
21 Laced pink p, *Dianthus*
22 Old cabbage rose s, *Rosa centifolia*
23 Globe artichoke p, *Cynara scolymus*
24 Lovage p, *Levisticum officinale*
25 Alba rose s, *Rosa alba* 'Celestial'
26 Bronze fennel p, *Foeniculum vulgare purpureum*
27 Southernwood p, *Artemisia arbrotanum*
28 Narcissus 'White Sail'
29 Damask rose s, *Rosa damascena* 'Omar Khayyam'
30 Lovage p, *Levisticum officinale*
31 Fennel p, *Foeniculum vulgare*
32 Apothecary's rose s, *Rosa gallica officinalis*
33 Thyme p, *Thymus*
34 Tulip b, *Tulipa* 'Rembrandt'
35 Rosemary p, *Rosmarinus officinalis*
36 Rue p, *Ruta graveolens*
37 Standard woodbine honeysuckle p, *Lonicera periclymenum*
38 Tulip b, *Tulipa* 'Rembrandt'
39 Sweetbriar Rose r, *Rosa rubiginosa* 'Amy Robsart'

Section 4

A Small crescent bed nearest the sundial

1 Ginger mint p, *Mentha x gentilis* 'Variegata'

2 Standard woodbine honeysuckle s, *Lonicera periclymenum*
3 Pot majoram p, *Origanum onites*
4 Standard woodbine honeysuckle s, *Lonicera periclymenum*
5 Thyme p, *Thymus*

B Middle crescent bed

1 Pot marigold a, *Calendula officinalis*
2 Curry plant p, *Helichrysum angustifolium*
3 Tulip b, *Tulipa chrysantha*
4 Iris reticulata b, *Iris reticulata* 'J S Dijt'
5 Rose s, *Rosa*
6 Wild majoram p, *Origanum vulgare*
7 Pineapple mint p, *Mentha rotundifolia variegata*
8 Lavender p, *Lavandula*
9 Provins rose s, *Rosa gallica* 'Versicolor' syn. 'Rosa Mundi'
10 Laced pink p, *Dianthus*
11 Thyme p, *Thymus praecox*
12 Rose s, *Rosa* 'Tricolor de Flanders'
13 Cotton lavender p, *Santolina virens*
14 Tricolour sage p, *Salvia officinalis* 'Tricolor'
15 Cabbage rose s, *Rosa centifolia* 'De Meaux'
16 Golden garlic b, *Allium moly*
17 Lemon balm p, *Melissa officinalis*
18 Tulip b, *Tulipa clusiana*

C Large corner bed

1 Sweetbriar rose s, *Rosa rubiginosa* 'Meg Merrilees'
2 Wild jonquil b, *Narcissus jonquila* 'Trevithian'
3 Rosemary p, *Rosmarinus officinalis*
4 Standard woodbine honeysuckle p, *Lonicera periclymenum*
5 Cotton lavender p, *Santolina chamaecyparissus*
6 English mace p, *Achillea decolorans*
7 Provins rose r, *Rosa gallica* 'Jenny Duval'
8 Horse mint p, *Mentha longifolia*
9 Laced pink p, *Dianthus*
10 Fragrant thyme p, *Thymus odoratissimus*
11 Tree onion b, *Allium cepa proliferum*
12 Polyanthus p, *Primula* 'Gold Laced'

13 Golden sage p, *Salvia officinalis* 'Icterina'
14 Old cabbage rose s, *Rosa centifolia*
15 Hyssop p, *Hyssopus officinalis*
16 Provins rose s, *Rosa gallica* 'Versicolor' syn. 'Rosa Mundi'
17 Lavender p, *Lavandula spica*
18 Rose s, *Rosa* 'Earl of Dufferin'
19 Dwarf artemisia p, *Artemisia schmidtiana*
20 Golden lemon balm p, *Melissa officinalis* 'Aurea'
21 Tulip b, *Tulipa* 'Dr Plesman'
22 Laced pink p, *Dianthus*
23 French tarragon p, *Artemisia dracunculus*
24 Provins rose s, *Rosa gallica* 'Hyppolyte'
25 Alba Rose s, *Rosa alba* 'Maiden's Blush'
26 Globe artichoke p, *Cynara scolymus*
27 Southernwood p, *Artemisia abrotanum*
28 Evening primrose p, *Oenothera biennis*
29 Tulip b, *Tulipa* 'Rembrandt'
30 Tulip b, *Tulipa marjoletii*
31 Bistort p, *Polygonum bistorta*
32 Purple sage p, *Salvia officinalis* 'Purpurascens'
33 Apothecary's rose s, *Rosa gallica officinalis*
34 Common mullein p, *Verbascum thapsiforme*
35 Alba rose s, *Rosa alba* 'Celestial'
36 Rosemary p, *Rosmarinus officinalis*
37 Lovage p, *Levisticum officinale*
38 Damask rose s, *Rosa damscena* 'Omar Khayyam'
39 Narcissus b, *Narcissus* 'White Sail'
40 Standard woodbine honeysuckle p, *Lonicera periclymenum*
41 Sweetbriar rose r, *Rosa rubiginosa* 'Amy Robsart'
42 Costmary p, *Chrysanthemum balsamita* (formerly *Tanacetum balsamita*)
43 Sweet cicely p, *Myrrhis odorata*

Around the sundial

1 Creeping chamomile p, *Chamaemelum nobile* 'Treneague'
2 Thyme p, *Thymus praecox*

Bordering the paths

1 Lavender p, *Lavandula spica* 'Munstead'

2 Chives p, *Allium schoenoprasum*
4 London pride p, *Saxifraga urbicum*

Roses hedging the boundary beds
Sweetbriar rose s, *Rosa rubiginosa* 'Lady Penzance'

THE PRIORY COURTYARD HERB GARDEN AT LAVENHAM

The small Suffolk town of Lavenham is famed for its ancient timber-framed buildings and one of the most recently restored of these is The Priory. The medieval core of the present building was originally inhabited by Benedictine monks and it is the monks, rather than the wool merchants that later brought prosperity to the town, who have most influenced the theme of the courtyard garden. It was not until 1985, six years after Alan and Gwenneth Casey had bought the then derelict Priory, that they embarked on designing and planting the garden. The decision to make a herb garden rather than a conventional ornamental garden reflects an aspect of the monk's life, herb growing and usage being an important preoccupation of medieval religious communities. Herbs were used to make dyes, cleanse and sweeten the atmosphere, flavour food and perhaps most importantly, as healing agents. It was the Anglo-Saxon word *drigan*, which means to dry, which gave us the word drug, most medicinal herbs having been dried before use.

The design of the garden also has historic connections for the centre-piece is a five-pointed star. This was the emblem of the De Vere family, the Earls of Oxford, who were Lords of the Manor of Lavenham for nearly 600 years from the time of the Battle of Hastings (1066). Measuring 32 sq ft (3 sq m), the garden is bounded by yew hedges on two sides, and on the other two by the building and courtyard. Working from the centre of the garden, triangular beds surround the star fashioned out of flints, rectangular beds stud the paving of stable bricks, and large triangular beds, planted with tall dyeing, aromatic, medicinal or culinary herbs, soften the corners of the whole.

The relatively simple design, choice of plants and the manner in which they have been massed, rather than dotted, gives the garden an attractively bold and generous character. It also ensures that even in mid-winter there is something to admire. The sculpture of the monk with his head bowed and the addition of the sundial, a traditional feature of herb gardens, enhances the harmonious mix of the old and the new.

The ground is well drained and a considerable amount of sand and lime was added to the soil before it was planted and the paving laid. The herbs obviously relish these conditions for, despite never having been watered since they were planted, they flourish. They have stood up to unusually hot summers without wilting and have a surprisingly long flowering period. Their deliciously sweet and peppery scents, entrapped within the boundary walls and hedges, can be savoured at ground level or, along with a bird's eye view of the overall design, from the first-floor windows of The Priory itself.

HERBS GROWN IN THE PRIORY COURTYARD GARDEN
(a = annual, b = biennial, p = perennial)
Around the flint star
1 Thyme p, *Thymus serpyllum* 'Pink Chintz'
  2 Golden thyme p, *Thymus vulgaris* 'Aureus'
3 Creeping thyme p, *Thymus serpyllum*
4 Woolly thyme p, *Thymus* 'Desboro'
5 Creeping thyme p, *Thymus serpyllum albus* 'Snowdrift'

Rectangular beds
1 Rue p, *Ruta graveolens*
2 Roman wormwood p, *Artemisia pontica*
3 Lavender p, *Lavandula angustifolia* 'Hidcote'
4 Purple sage p, *Salvia officinalis* 'Purpurascens'
5 Cotton lavender p, *Santolina chamaecyparissus*

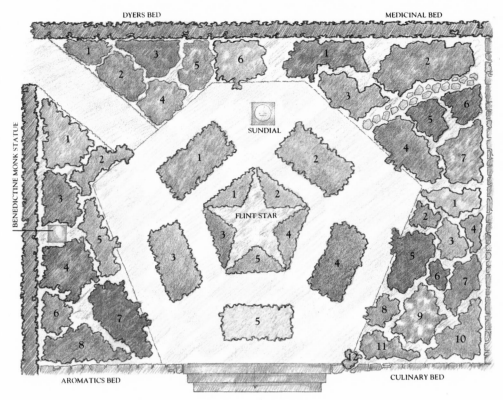

Dyer's bed
1 Roman chamomile p, *Chamaemelum nobile*
2 Tansy p, *Tanacetum vulgare*
3 Woad b, *Isatis tinctoria*
4 Lady's bedstraw p, *Galium verum*
5 Woodruff p, *Asperula odorata*
6 Fennel p, *Foeniculum vulgare*

Medicinal bed
1 Wormwood p, *Artemisia absinthium*
2 Rosemary p, *Rosmarinus officinalis*
3 Wild or creeping thyme p, *Thymus serpyllum*
4 Purple sage p, *Salvia officinalis* 'Purpurascens'
5 Roman chamomile p, *Chamaemelum nobile*
6 Borage a, *Borago officinalis*
7 Jacob's ladder p, *Polemonium caeruleum*

Aromatic's bed
1 Mountain balm p, *Calamintha officinalis*

Opposite
The sun-baked Priory Garden, Lavenham.

2 Lavender p, *Lavandula*
3 Rosemary p, *Rosmarinus officinalis*
4 Marjorams (various) p, *Origanum*
5 Thymes (various) p, *Thymus*
6 Cotton lavender p, *Santolina chamaecyparissus*
7 Hyssop p, *Hyssopus officinalis*
8 Bergamot p, *Monarda didyma*

Culinary bed
1 Thyme p, *Thymus vulgaris*
2 Sage p, *Salvia officinalis*
3 Welsh onion b, *Allium fistulosum*
4 Chives p, *Allium schoenoprasum*
5 Parsley b, *Petroselinum crispum*
6 Italian parsley b, *Petroselinum neapolitanum*
7 Marjoram p, *Origanum*
8 Celeriac a, *Apium graveolens*
9 Wild strawberries p, *Fragaria vesca*
10 Chicory p, *Cichorium intybus*
11 Lemon balm p, *Melissa officinalis*
12 Fennel p *Feoniculum vulgare*

Useful Addresses

Organizations

The Herb Society
PO Box 415
London SW1P 2HE
(Write enclosing SAE)

National Institute of Medical Herbalists
41 Hatherley Road
Winchester
Hampshire

The Soil Association
86–88 Colston Street
Bristol BS1 5BB
Avon

Botanic gardens

Chelsea Physic Garden
66 Royal Hospital Road
London SW3

Royal Botanic Gardens
Kew
Richmond
Surrey

Good health food stores and chemists frequently stock
dried herbs and products such as essential oils.
Alternatively these products can be obtained from the
following outlets:

Baldwins
173 Walworth Road
London SE17

Culpeper
21 Bruton Street
Berkeley Square
London W1X 7DA (Many other branches
nationwide)
Mail order: Culpeper Ltd, Hadstock Road, Linton,
Cambridge CB1 6NJ

Gaia Natural Therapies
London Road
Forest Row
East Sussex RH18 5EZ

Little Herbs
1 West Street
Ware
Hertfordshire SG12 9EE

Neal's Yard Remedies
2 Neal's Yard
Covent Garden
London WC2 (Branches also in Oxford, and Totnes,
Devon)

Plants and seeds

John Chambers
15 Westleigh Road
Barton Seagrave
Kettering
Northamptonshire

Chanctonbury Herbs
104 High Street
Steyning
West Sussex BN4 3RD

Hollington Nurseries Ltd
Woolton Hill
Newbury
Berkshire

Iden Croft Herbs
Frittenden Road
Staplehurst
Kent TN12 0DN

Suffolk Herbs
Sawyers Farm
Little Cornard
Sudbury
Suffolk CO10 0NY

Sutton Seeds
Hele Road
Torquay
Devon TQ2 7QJ

Thompson and Morgan
London Road
Ipswich
Suffolk IP2 0BA

Addresses of featured gardens

Hatfield House
Hatfield
Hertfordshire AL9 5NF

Devon Herbs
Thorn Cottage
Burn Lane
Brentor
Tavistock
Devon PL19 0ND

Polyphant Herb Garden
Launceston
**(this garden
is not open
to the public)**

The Priory
Water Street
Lavenham
Suffolk CO10 9RW

The Tudor Garden
Bugle Street
Southampton
Hampshire

Useful addresses in the USA

The American Herb Association
PO Box 353
Rescue
California 95672

The Californian School of Herbal Studies
PO Box 39
9309 HWY 116
Forestville
California 95436

The Dominion Herbal College
7527 Kingsway
Burnaby
BC Canada U3N–3C1

FURTHER READING

A Modern Herbal, Mrs M Grieve, edited and introduced by Mrs C F Leyel. Penguin.
The Complete New Herbal, Richard Mabey. Elm Tree Books.
Culpeper Colour Herbal, edited by David Potterton. W Foulsham.
The Home Herbal, Barbara Griggs. Pan Books.
The A–Z of Modern Herbalism: A Comprehensive Guide to Practical Herbal Therapy, compiled and written by Simon Y Mills MA, FNIMH. Thorsons.
The Holistic Herbal, David Hoffman. Element Books.
Kitty Campion's Handbook of Herbal Health. Century Hutchinson.
Grandmother's Secrets, Jean Palaiseul. Penguin.
A Woman's Guide to Natural Beauty, Anita Guyton. Thorsons.
Herbal Cosmetics, Camilla Hepper. Thorsons.
The Herb Garden, Sarah Garland. Windward.
Herbs in the Garden, Allen Paterson. Dent.
Culpeper Guides:
Cooking with Herbs, Patricia Lousada. Webb & Bower/Michael Joseph.
Herbs and Aromatherapy, Joannah Metcalfe. Webb & Bower/Michael Joseph.
How to Grow Herbs, Ian Thomas. Webb & Bower/Michael Joseph.
Herbs and Health, Nicola Peterson. Webb & Bower/Michael Joseph.

ACKNOWLEDGEMENTS

The author and publishers would like to thank the organizations and people involved in the growing and use of herbs for their advice and information. Special thanks go to Simon McBride whose photographs illustrate the herb gardens, products and herb garden features. Thanks also to the owners of the gardens featured and Nicky and Michael Manisty, Caroline Weeks, Ian Thomas of Culpeper, Lynda Faulkner, Anna Gwilt ND,MRN,DO,MRO, and Rosalind Blackwell MNIMH for their assistance.

Notes on Illustrations

The A-Z Herbal illustrations have been chosen from:

Botanicum Medicinale (1759)
English Botany (1802)
English Herbal (16th century)
Flora Danica
Flora Graeca (1802)
Flora Medica (1829)
Flora Londinensis (1817)
Getreue Darstellung und Beschreibung der in der Arzneykund begrauchlichen Gewachse (1805)
Herbier de la France (1784)
Hours of Anney Burgundy (16th century)
Insects and Plants (1780)
La Botanique Mise à la Portée de Tout le Monde (1774)
Medical Botany (1831)
Medicinal Plants (1880)
Photographie Medicale

Picture Credits

ET Archive 31, 35, 36, 39, 43, 46, 49, 52, 55, 70, 76, 79, 81, 84, 86, 94, 102.

The Linnean Society 48, 58, 61, 63, 65, 67, 72, 74, 88, 92, 98.

Simon McBride Front jacket, back jacket, title page 11, 17, 22/3, 27, 104/5, 107, 108, 110, 115, 117, 119, 122, 123, 128, 132/3, 138.